Between Earth and Sky

Between Earth and Sky

POETS OF THE COWBOY WEST

Edited by Anne Heath Widmark

Photographs by Kent Reeves

Foreword by Kim R. Stafford

W. W. Norton & Company

LONDON · NEW YORK

Copyright © 1995 by Anne Heath Widmark
Photographs of Kent Reeves used with permission of the photographer
All rights reserved
Printed in the United States of America
First Edition

The text of this book is composed in Janson
with the display set in Latin Condensed & Matrix Wide
Composition by Crane Typesetting Service, Inc.
Manufacturing by the Courier Companies, Inc.
Book design by Chris Welch

Library of Congress Cataloging-in-Publication Data

Between earth and sky : poets of the cowboy West / edited by Anne
    Heath Widmark ; photographs by Kent Reeves ; foreword by Kim R.
    Stafford.
        p.   cm.
        1. American poetry—20th century.   2. Cowboys—West (U.S.)—
    Poetry.   I. Widmark, Anne Heath.   II. Reeves, Kent.
    PS615.B48   1995
    811′.540803278—dc20   94-40343

ISBN 0-393-03736-3

W. W. Norton & Company, Inc., 500 Fifth Avenue, New York, N.Y. 10110
W. W. Norton & Company Ltd., 10 Coptic Street, London WC1A 1PU

1 2 3 4 5 6 7 8 9 0

To my mother and father, with love

Contents

Foreword

The poems in this book braid us back to essential things. These poems map the tough weather on a hat time has bruised, and comb fingers through mane hair, and drape an arm over a horse's dusty back, and reach to speak tough losses, along with grit and humor and compassion. These poems are filled with moments that brand the mind, and this book is graced with photographs to double the punch. In these poems and images we go to the beginning, we follow the magic tunnel of our language back to the first sunrise, the daily achievement of good work.

If we read the oldest poem in the English language, a chant from around 400 A.D. called by scholars the *Gnomic Verses*, we find a list of plain certainties from nature, facts that ask no argument but fit to the rhythm of life. "Trout shall turn in a pool," say these lines, "and a storm shall gather, and a man shall be generous among his friends." The forward link of the poem is the word "and." One thing, and then another, and then another, all in the weave of natural time and the chant of a settled poetic line. In this spirit, I read the poems of this book's gathering.

The American poet William Carlos Williams called for a modern way of writing that featured "no ideas but in things." Don't we have that here? These are not poems of airy philosophy, but of experience rooted to saddle and hoof, glove and rock. Williams also said that while poetry doesn't always sell, people die every day for the need of it. People cave in, turn aside, back off from their lives. When it's made well, poetry can call us to our best endeavor: see, feel, remember, and ride the pleasure of right living.

These poets have lived something in the open. They have been hospitable to a multitude of little knowings that add up to abundance. There is a wholeness of experience, a circling over native ground, insights and plain sense. And once that feel is complete, then the words of the poem, the heartbeat of its making, start through the gate, and become this chanted song, this stream of words that have grown comfortable in their arrangement stepping forward along the path. It is their gathering that made it work, the harboring of observation over time until the herd is ready, and then the counting out through the gate in a living trail of words.

Kim R. Stafford

Introduction

In January 1992, at the eighth annual Cowboy Poetry Gathering in Elko, Nevada, I first heard Buck Ramsey recite "Anthem." A prologue to a sixty-four-page ballad, the poem tells of the early cowboy's deep-felt communion with the land and all it holds. As I watched the solitary figure spotlighted onstage and listened to the beauty of the words spoken in Buck's gentle Texas drawl, the imagery and cadence of that majestic poem, I felt a sense of recognition, of homecoming. That evening a seed was planted. "Anthem" became the inspiration for this book.

I soon discovered that this sense of homecoming had been experienced by the poets themselves during Elko's first Cowboy Poetry Gathering, organized in 1985 by a group of Western States folklorists headed by Hal Cannon, director of the Western Folklife Center. Living on isolated ranches, most of the poets had never met before. The sudden connection with one another, the sharing of poems and stories which up until then had been their secret, private language, was like a family reunion.

Despite an exploding popularity—each year thousands brave bitter winter temperatures to attend the event—the atmosphere of good-humored camaraderie, of acceptance rather than competition, has, for the most part, prevailed. Speaking of the "family" of poets that has emerged from that first

Gathering, Vess Quinlan told me, "I've never been around such talented people with such gentle egos."

The Elko Gathering—and the over one hundred gatherings it has spawned—has provided a place to preserve and revive the cowboy culture, and to celebrate a uniquely enduring way of life. Cowboy poetry is an oral tradition of the West that was born during the long trail drives of the 1800s. Sitting around their campfires, cowboys began a tradition of storytelling, poetry, and song that has survived on ranches from Texas to Montana and is now undergoing a modern renaissance, both in oral performance and as written literature.

The twelve poets in *Between Earth and Sky* are part of a vital literary movement taking place in the American West. In voices as diverse as the individuals themselves, these poets speak to, and from, the soul of a people who remain intimately connected to the rhythms of land, animals, and seasons. Their poems grow out of a lifetime of shared, hands-on experience, a history of friends, family and effort, of neighbors helping neighbors with branding, gathering, and other chores—all rooted in a sense of place.

Like their predecessors, today's cowboys, ranchers, and bronc riders exist—in fact, are most truly *alive*—in the vast physical and metaphorical space between earth and sky. Their livelihood brings them close to the heart of being: to moments of life and death, the grace of simple beauty, and the profound drama of natural phenomena. It is a life conducive to poetry.

With honest emotion, eloquence, and wit, the poets gathered here render the textures of a way of life increasingly endangered by the pressures of modern times. The West, which has been home to generations of ranching families, is under siege as different factions—environmentalists, government agencies, and private landowners—battle over a rapidly diminishing landscape. Today, less than two percent of Americans live on farms and ranches, tied to a slower, more natural lifestyle that is fast disappearing. There is ingrained in the sensibility of the West a lingering sense of loss. Yet, with the economic struggles now threatening the ranching community, there has been this extraordinary resurgence of poetry—not the academic variety, but poetry as song: wordmusic. At a recent gathering, Wyoming poet Bill Jones remarked, "Maybe the only way we can keep this way of life alive is to write poems about it."

In preserving the old stories, rooted in the ways of the cow camp, traditionalists among cowboy poets adhere to the narrative ballad form of metered and rhymed verse. Both the sentiment and the music of their poems derive from the Spanish—"the loving tongue," as early cowboy poet Badger Clark called it—brought to the West by Mexican vaqueros, the original cowboys. In recent years, there has been an exhilarating and broadly accepted expansion into new styles of form and content. While maintaining the distinctive cowboy vernacular, what Wallace McRae terms "the lingo of our calling," more poets are trying to tell a new story, to free the cowboy from stereotypes of the past, and to write the poems of modern ranching and rodeo experience. "Our poems," McRae says, "tell how it is for us today, right here."

Though cowboy poetry is historically male dominated, the contemporary movement includes a growing number of stirring female voices, women who share the work of cowboying "stirrup to stirrup" with the men. In cattle country, "cowboy" is not gender specific: a good hand is a good hand. As more and more Western women write their stories, riding free over the range of human experience, they are expanding the emotional and poetic landscape.

Reaching far beyond its cow-country beginnings, the poetry of the cowboy West is awakening a response in mainstream America. In today's restless, virtual-reality society there is a yearning for things of intrinsic worth: for a connection to the land, for the sound of the human voice, for simple, natural truth. We are trying to find the way home.

Between Earth and Sky represents my own trail "home," a return to the terrain of my childhood. At age four, I learned to ride on an old pinto mare and later spent my happiest days horseback on my family's working ranch in Hidden Valley, California. Those early years engendered a lifelong affinity for animals and open country, and the skilled, quiet ways of the cowboys who worked on the valley's ranches made a lasting impression. At the same time, I grew up uniquely close to the popular image of the cowboy, as portrayed by my father in Hollywood westerns. While my attraction to cowboys as heroic figures has remained, I wanted to learn more about the actual people and the real lives that have steadfastly existed a world away from the romanticized stereotype.

This, then, was my starting point. Inspired by "Anthem," and in collaboration with photographer Kent Reeves, I embarked on the creation of this book, a process which became a personal odyssey.

My odyssey began in southeastern Montana, with a visit to our first poet, Wallace McRae. As Kent and I bumped along in Wally's pickup over the unbroken rangeland of his Rocker Six ranch, Montana's "poet lariat" entertained us with poems and stories; and, with his gift for mimicry and dialect, he reenacted scenes from a play he'd recently performed at the community theatre in Colstrip. Storytelling and reciting poetry, usually partnered with humor, come as naturally to cowboy poets as moving to the rhythm of a horse's gait.

Before dinner with Wally's family, I went for a walk. The evening light was turning the grass to gold and there were dark clouds over the horizon. A small herd of antelope grazed in the shadow of a nearby butte. Wally's dog, Maggie, couldn't resist and gave chase. As the animals gracefully retreated, there was hardly a sound—only the ceaseless whispering of the wind across the plains. On the way back, a group of curious horses gathered on a hill, silhouetted against the sky: a scene out of a Charles M. Russell painting. And this was just the beginning.

During the ensuing months, Kent and I traveled the West, visiting poets from the northern ranges of Montana to the lonely breaks of the Texas Panhandle and the immense grassland of southwestern New Mexico. With each visit, we found a life and a loved place known clear to the bone. And we discovered complex, multifaceted people who, in addition to being poets and cowboys, are performers and musicians, short-story and essay writers, artists, teachers, parents, humorists, veterans, historians, preservationists, and more.

With a hospitality typical of those who follow the cowboy code, the poets and their families welcomed us into their homes, sharing food, philosophy, stories, laughter, and occasionally misfortune. During these encounters I was continually moved by the warmth and friendship extended to us. Not a true insider to cowboy culture, I was amazed at how quickly bonds are formed when people share common values and are simply real with one another.

Almost exactly one year after that first visit with Wally McRae, I again found myself driving over rugged terrain—this time in southwestern New Mexico, in Drum Hadley's Land Rover. Moving through the awesome, mysterious expanse of the Gray Ranch, I listened as another poet cowboy told stories and recited, at times in "the loving tongue," lines from his poems. In the sounds of the words I heard the language of the land, and the voices of the vaqueros who'd lived and cowboyed there. In one seamless moment, I grasped how, like braided rawhide, land, animals, weather, people, stories, songs, poems, all are interwoven. One strand cannot be lost without losing the whole.

By traveling deeper into western landscapes, by coming to know the inhabitants, and by listening to the precision and beauty—the music—of cowboys' speech, I *lived* the rhythms of their poems. I encountered what they experience every day and voice in poetry: a communion of the human and the natural, a kind of felt wisdom, dictated by the heart. I had circled back to "Anthem," and to my own rural beginnings.

The current surge of interest in the West indicates that in these troubled times we're returning to our Western mythology, and particularly to cowboys as embodiments of basic American ideals. But we need a better story than the one we've been telling about the West, and we need new kinds of heroes. In *Owning It All*, William Kittredge tells us that there is a new candor afoot in the land, an "impulse to see straight to the beating heart of things." It is this impulse, I believe, that is drawing so many to the poetry of the cowboy West and to the remarkable people who create it.

Anne Heath Widmark

"The real soul of America is in its land and people close to the land."

Ellen Cotton, rancher

"No place is a place until it has had a poet."

Wallace Stegner

Buck Ramsey

"The cowboy way has been lost for generations, and we're just now
rediscovering it through traditional cowboy poetry and songs.
We're finding our voice again, and the traditional forms give us an opportunity
for re-identifying with the cowboy calling."

Bonnie Trina

She was giving birth to her first child when Bonnie Trina died,
All the leaves were out, the trees were full of flowers.
She had known the Fiddle all her life, had two years been his bride,
But the time had seemed more like a few good hours.

There was mention of some neighborly assistance with the birth,
But she wanted only Fiddle—then the child.
He had felt her thrilling pangs and had felt her painful mirth,
He had felt her cries and failed to feel her smile.

He had felt his whole world tumbling down when Bonnie Trina died,
And the boy brought little to his breaking heart.
No one ever knew, would ever know, how much or if he cried,
Ever know how deep the dying made its mark.

In the darkness of the morning he came knocking at the door
Of a neighbor place two hour's ride away.
"Could you tend this boy?" he asked the wife, and muttered little more
As the morning sun came bringing on the day.

While the woman tended to the child as if it were her own,
Fiddle and the man warmed hands around their coffee.
In a while he spoke, "I reckon we will lay our Bonnie down
In the river grove." The Fiddle spoke so softly.

"You recall we planned to gather from the river in the morning
For some sortin' and to count and move the yearlings.
So we'll meet there at the river for our Bonnie's next sojourning.
Maybe you could do the proper sermoneerings.

"Tell the boys to bring their horses that they gather pastures on
And we'll gather out that pasture from the river.
I'll just leave her where I loved her best. It's better done at dawn.
That's the kind of fare-thee-well she'd have us give her."

So they gathered at the river and they buried her at dawn
By a meadow, beneath cottonwood, full leaf.
"She shall be in league with rocks of fields . . ." The speaking wasn't long.

Then they pulled their cinches, rode off with their grief.

As he told off all the riders and they dropped off on the drag,
Fiddle dropped the gray with Bonnie Trina's saddle.
When they gathered to the common hold, the gray came with a jag—
About as many as the other riders' cattle.

Through the day as Fiddle made the cuts, the gray turned back the herd
At the place where he was posted on the hold.
When the work was done, the boys all loosed their cinches and lingered.

Each would know his leaving time and not be told.

Fiddle turned his blue roan loose and placed his saddle by the barn,
And he loosed the gray and laid that saddle by.
When he laid his head down on his own and wrapped hers in an arm,
All the boys knew leaving time was drawing nigh.

Fiddle sleeps and Bonnie rests, and all the boys have taken leave,
And the horses, two, untethered seem to tarry.
And the baby boy is lying still and growing at his ease.
And the cattle scatter out upon the prairie.

Anthem

And in the morning I was riding
Out through the breaks of that long plain,
And leather creaking in the quieting
Would sound with trot and trot again.
I lived in time with horse hoof falling;
I listened well and heard the calling
The earth, my mother bade to me,
Though I would still ride wild and free.
And as I flew out on the morning
Before the bird, before the dawn,
I was the poem, I was the song.
My heart would beat the world a warning—
Those horsemen now rode all with me,
And we were good and we were free.

We were not told, but ours the knowing
We were the native strangers there
Among the things of prairie growing—
This knowing gave us more the care
To let the grass keep at its growing
And let the streams keep at their flowing.
We knew the land would not be ours,
That no one has the awful powers
To claim the vast and common nesting,
To own the life that gave him birth,
Much less to rape his Mother Earth
And ask her for a mother's blessing,
And ever live in peace with her,
And, dying, come to rest with her.

Oh, we would ride and we would listen
And hear the message on the wind.
The grass in morning dew would glisten
Until the sun would dry and blend
The grass to ground and air to skying.
We'd know by bird or insect flying,

Or by their mood or by their song,
If time and moon were right or wrong
For fitting works and rounds to weather.
The critter coats and leaves of trees
Might flash some signal with a breeze—
Or wind and sun on flow'r or feather.
We knew our way from dawn to dawn,
And far beyond, and far beyond.

It was the old ones with me riding
Out through the fog fall of the dawn,
And they would press me to deciding
If we were right or we were wrong.
For time came we were punching cattle
For men who knew not spur nor saddle,
Who came with locusts in their purse
To scatter loose upon the earth.
The savage had not found this prairie
Till some who hired us came this way
To make the grasses pay and pay
For some raw greed no wise or wary
Regard for grass could satisfy.
The old ones wept, and so did I.

Do you remember? We'd come jogging
To town with jingle in our jeans,
And in the wild night we'd be bogging
Up to our hats in last month's dreams.
It seemed the night could barely hold us
With all those spirits to embold us
While, horses waiting on three legs,
We'd drain the night down to the dregs.
And just before beyond redemption
We'd gather back to what we were,
We'd leave the money left us there
And head our horses for the wagon.
But in the ruckus, in the whirl,
We were the wolves of all the world.

The grass was growing scarce for grazing,
Would soon turn sod or soon turn bare.

The money men set to replacing
The good and true in spirit there.
We could not say, there was no knowing,
How ill the future winds were blowing.
Some cowboys even shunned the ways
Of cowboys in the trail-herd days,
(But where's the gift not turned for plunder?)
Forgot that we are what we do
And not the stuff we lay claim to.
I dream the spell that we were under—
I throw in with a cowboy band
And go out horseback through the land.

So mornings now I'll go out riding
Through pastures of my solemn plain,
And leather creaking in the quieting
Will sound with trot and trot again.
I'll live in time with horse hoof falling,
I'll listen well and hear the calling
The earth, my mother, bids to me,
Though I will still ride wild and free.
And as I fly out on the morning
Before the bird, before the dawn,
I'll be this poem, I'll be this song.
My heart will beat the world a warning—
Those horsemen will ride all with me,
And we'll be good, and we'll be free.

BUCK RAMSEY

Buck Ramsey did what he calls the best part of his growing up in the Texas Panhandle, along the north rim of the Canadian River Breaks, where the flat and level plains drop away in a jumble of washes and draws down to the distant river. North and across the river from Amarillo, about midway between the towns of Channing and Dumas, is the site of Buck's favorite boyhood home. As far as the eye can see, in all directions, is a landscape of buffalo and gramma grasses, dotted with mesquite, cholla, sage, and yucca. "This country is wholly unstifling to the spirit," Buck says. "It doesn't crowd you in." He calls this region, with its expansive, mystical quality, "my heart's country."

He was born in 1938 to a family of cotton farmers, and his family, as Buck says, "blessedly" moved from the cotton country of the south plains to the wheat and cattle country of the north plains while he was still an infant. While he was in grade school, the family moved to the ranch country north of the river. This was where Buck began his love affair with cowboy life, going horseback and often rambling on foot through the Canadian River Breaks to visit cowboys on neighboring ranches. As a boy, he started earning wages horseback, punching cows on the Tierra Blanca, the Bryant Cattle Company, the Turkey Tracks, and the Cold Water Cattle Company.

In the midst of what is increasingly corporate-owned ranch and farmland stands what is left of the red-brick, two-room schoolhouse where Buck got what he considers the best of his education. Buck wrote his first poems in that little grade school in Middlewell. He also began what became a lifetime of self-directed learning that has ranged from Aristotle and Plato, Camus and Pirsig, to Russian and American literature, to poets—the traditional cowboy variety as well as moderns such as Wallace Stevens, T. S. Eliot, and A. E. Housman. As for formal education, Buck called it quits after high school in Amarillo. Like many self-educated people, his erudition ranges as wide and free as his curiosity.

Just before turning twenty-five years old, newly married and with a child on the way, Buck, while working as a roughstock rider and general cowhand on the Cold Water Cattle Company, was "on the losing end of an altercation with a spoiled, sorry horse named Cinnamon." As a result of some gear tearing apart and "just landing wrong," he ended up getting around in a wheelchair.

Soon after basic rehabilitation from his injury, Buck went to work as a newspaper reporter for the *Amarillo Daily News* and *The Globe Times* and soon graduated into magazine writing. Beginning in the late sixties he began contributing articles and essays to the *Texas Observer*, a liberal fortnightly journal published in Austin. When one of its editors, the prominent Texas populist Jim Hightower, entered the political arena in the early eighties, Buck signed on to do press relations and some speech writing.

With his wife Bette, a teacher and counselor whom he met in high school, Buck now lives in a homey Old English-style house on a tree-lined street in Amarillo. Not surprisingly, the house is filled with books and cowboy artifacts. Buck has never quit being a cowboy. Working cowboys—members of the "cowboy tribe," as Buck calls them—treat him as one of their own, and defer without question to his authority on matters of cowboy lore and, most of all, on matters of the cowboy spirit.

That cowboy spirit, Buck holds, is inextricably linked to a communion with the earth. "I think cowboys are the true environmentalists of the West. The early cowboys loved the grass and were close to the land. Much like the Indian. Charley Russell, one of my heroes, used to say, 'a cowboy is just a white Indian.' This is what 'Anthem' deals with."

"Central to the cowboy way is its cult of skill—it's what you can do that counts, not what you can get." Contrary to the image of cowboys as rugged individualists, Buck says that "cowpunching is wholly a nurturing occupation—birthing and tending. All of cowboys' skills are turned to husbandry. They may not admit it, but calving heifers—with all its sleepless vigilance and cold, bone-aching drudgery—is the favorite task of many a wild and woolly, bronc-stomping, fancy-roping cowpuncher."

Buck claims that the current resurgence of cowboy poetry is helping to bring back these sustaining values. He sees the movement as an opportunity for the cowboy tribe to "take its image and story away from the commercial hucksters, to present to the world the real version rather than the Hollywood, New York, and Nashville version."

Though Buck is best known as a poet, the unmistakable cadence of his poems stems from his rich musical heritage: "I had four sisters who sang as a gospel quartet, and we grew up in the old shape-note, Sacred Harp, four-part harmony gospel singing." This, together with his early exposure to and involvement with traditional cowboy songs, his honky-tonk days around country and swing, and a layman's appreciation for jazz and classical, have shaped his musical and poetic ear.

At poetry gatherings and at a variety of other venues, Buck sings in a pure, clear voice while accompanying himself on guitar, charming audiences with his easy, unassuming style. He is known for unembellished renditions of traditional cowboy songs such as "The Santa Fe Trail," "Goodbye, Old Paint," and "The Cowboy's Soliloquy." Buck's mission, he says, is to archive and record traditional cowboy music. His album, *Riding Uphill from Texas*, won the prestigious Wrangler Award for Outstanding Traditional Western Music at the 1993 Western Heritage Awards ceremonies at the National Cowboy Hall of Fame. In early 1994, he released another album, *My Home It Was in Texas.*

On a warm summer afternoon Kent and I, along with Bette, accompanied Buck on a drive through the Panhandle and a visit to Middlewell. At a ranch headquarters outside Channing we picked up a passenger, Rooster Morris, whom Buck introduced as "the best fiddle player around." On the way back to Amarillo, I asked Buck if Kent might photograph him against the wide landscape of his homeland. Soon Buck pulled his converted van off the highway, over a cattle guard and onto a dirt road. "I used to cowboy on this outfit—they may throw us out," he said with a mischievous grin.

Less than a quarter mile down the road we found an ideal spot. When Buck and Rooster had taken their places beside a barbed-wire fence, instruments in hand, two pickups drove up and stopped in a swirl of dust. A family of working cowboys, including a woman and two young boys, climbed out and greeted Buck enthusiastically. They were old friends, on their way home from a long day of branding. With the unexpected audience assembled on truck hoods, and as the sun slipped behind the far horizon, an impromptu concert began. No one seemed surprised when a group of roving coyotes joined in for the chorus. Bette said that such magic often occurs when Buck's around.

These days Buck spends almost half the year on the road, reciting poetry and singing to appreciative audiences. And he continues to write eloquent, powerful pieces ranging from poetry to essays to short stories. In all, his roots remain. "Everything I write," he says, "comes out of Middlewell, the place and the people of my childhood."

Wallace McRae

"We think that our way of life is important . . .
Who's going to tell our story?
Who's going to get across the way
we feel to other people?"

Things of Intrinsic Worth

Remember that sandrock on Emmels Crick
Where Dad carved his name in 'thirteen?
It's been blasted down into rubble
And interred by their dragline machine.
Where Fadhls lived, at the old Milar Place,
Where us kids stole melons at night?
They 'dozed it up in a funeral pyre
Then torched it. It's gone alright.
The "C" on the hill, and the water tanks
Are now classified "reclaimed land."
They're thinking of building a golf course
Out there, so I understand.
The old Egan Homestead's an ash pond
That they say is eighty feet deep.
The branding corral at the Douglas Camp
Is underneath a spoil heap.
And across the crick is a tipple, now,
Where they load coal onto a train.
The Mae West Rock on Hay Coulee?
Just black-and-white snapshots remain.
There's a railroad loop and a coal storage shed
Where the bison kill site used to be.
The Guy Place is gone; Ambrose's too.
Beulah Farley's a ranch refugee.

But things are booming. We've got this new school
That's envied across the whole state.
When folks up and ask, "How things goin' down there?"
I grin like a fool and say, "Great!"
Great God, how we're doin'! We're rollin' in dough,
As they tear and they ravage The Earth.
And nobody knows . . . or nobody cares . . .
About things of intrinsic worth.

Little Things

I've laid for hours upon my back
Just looking at the sky,
At clouds, or if the sky was clear,
The motes within my eye.
D'ja ever spend an hour or more
Just staring at the crick?
Or a scarab roll a ball of dung?
Or ants rasslin' with a stick?
Or, on a cloudy, windy day,
See a windmill seem to fall?
Or stop stock still with neck hairs raised
By a plaintive coyote call?
Swallows slice their swaths across
The sky like scimitars.
I'm humbled by the intricate
Snowflakes' prismic stars.
I've laughed as stove-top killdeer
Go a-scrabblin' 'cross a draw.
I've seen cedar trees explode in flames
As I'm consumed with awe.
Arms crossed and leaning forward,
Weight on the saddle horn,
I'm a fascinated crowd of one;
A calf is being born.

The measure of your intellect,
The learn-ed people say,
Are the things that fascinate us.
They're a mental exposé.
You got to be dang careful
If you want to be thought smart,
And keep sorta confidential
Little things that's in your heart.

Reincarnation

"What does reincarnation mean?"
A cowpoke ast his friend.
His pal replied, "It happens when
Yer life has reached its end.
They comb yer hair, and wash yer neck,
And clean yer fingernails,
And lay you in a padded box
Away from life's travails.

"The box goes in a hole
That's been dug in the ground.
Reincarnation starts in when
Yore planted 'neath a mound.
Them clods melt down, just like yer box,
And you who is inside.
And then yore just beginnin' on
Yer transformation ride.

"In a while, the grass'll grow
Upon yer rendered mound.
Till some day on yer moldered grave
A lonely flower is found.
And say a hoss should wander by,
And gaze upon this flower,
That once wuz you, but now's become
Yer vegetative bower.

"The posy that the hoss done ate
Up, with his other feed,
Makes bone, and fat, and muscle
Essential to the steed.
But some is left that he can't use,
And so it passes through,
And finally lays upon the ground.
This thing, that once wuz you.

"Then say, by chance, I wanders by,
And sees this on the ground.
And I ponders, and I wonders at,
This object that I found.
I thinks of reincarnation,
Of life, and death, and such.
I come away concludin': 'Slim,
You ain't changed all that much.' "

We Never Rode the Judiths

For Ian Tyson

We never rode the Judiths when we were gray-wolf wild.
Never gathered Powder River, Palo Duro, or John Day.
No, we never rode the Judiths when their sirens preened and smiled.
And we'll never ride the Judiths before they carry us away.

Cowboys cut for sign on back trails to the days that used to be
Sorting, sifting through chilled ashes of the past.
Or focused on some distant star, out near eternity,
Always hoping that the next day will be better than the last.

Out somewhere in the future, where spring grass is growing tall,
We rosin up our hopes for bigger country, better pay.
But as the buckers on our buckles grow smooth-mouthed
   or trip and fall
We know tomorrow's draw ain't gonna throw no gifts our way.

And we never rode the Judiths when we were gray-wolf bold.
Never rode the Grande Ronde Canyon out north of Enterprise.
No we never rode the Judiths, and we know we're getting old
As old trails grow steeper, longer, right before our eyes.

My horses all are twenty-some . . . ain't no good ones coming on.
The deejays and the Nashville Hands won't let ". . . Amazed"
   turn gold.
We're inclined to savor evening now. We usta favor dawn.
Seems we're not as scared of dyin' as we are of growing old.

I wish we'd a' rode the Judiths when we were gray-wolf wild.
And gathered Powder River, Palo Duro, and John Day.
But we never rode the Judiths when their sirens' songs beguiled
And we'll never ride the Judiths before they carry us away.

WALLACE McRAE

The McRae family is in the fifth generation ranching on Rosebud Creek, just south of Colstrip, Montana. Wallace McRae's grandfather came from Lochalsh, Scotland, to southeastern Montana in 1882. After losing all his sheep during the infamous winter of 1886–1887, John B. McRae sold the pelts in order to purchase the 160 acres that started the McRae ranch. The Rocker Six Cattle Company is now 30,000 acres. "It's a two-man operation," Wally says. Wally and Clint, the oldest of his three children, work the place alone, trading help with neighbors for branding and the fall roundup.

Known as the "cowboy curmudgeon," a title fully in keeping with his own self-image, Wally is a multifaceted man with a breadth of knowledge and talent. Among the many hats he wears are rancher, poet, humorist, philosopher, cultural preservationist, and thespian. Wally studied theater in college. For the past ten years, he's been an active member of a local theater group, the Coal and Cattle Country Players, as actor, director, lyricist, and playwright. He is a featured performer at the annual Cowboy Poetry Gathering in Elko, and he has recited his poems regularly on the syndicated TV show, *The West*. In 1990 Wally became the first cowboy poet to be granted a National Heritage Award from the National Endowment for the Arts. Fellow poet Baxter Black has said of his good friend, "Were he from any other country on earth, Wallace McRae would be a national treasure."

Wally was born in 1936 in Miles City. After receiving a degree in zoology from Montana State University in 1958, he joined the Navy and traveled the world. While stationed in Norfolk, Virginia, he met his wife, Ruth, and he began to long for the land he'd left behind. "I didn't appreciate this place—the richness of the culture and traditions of ranch life—until I went away from it and came back," he says. "I'd been blind to the poetry of my own roots."

The McRaes live in a part of the world where the nearest town, Colstrip, is fifteen miles away and the next, Lame Deer, is twenty-five miles farther south. Nothing in between but sky and land, nothing beyond but the Cheyenne reservation and the plain where Custer made his last stand. Describing those who live in the cowboy West, Wally has written, "We are envied and revered because we have room to ride, write, and swing a wide loop without whacking someone else in the hat brim or roping the neighbors' pug dog."

Several miles down a red dirt road, Wally and Ruth's ranch house is set into a hill overlooking Rosebud Creek. They designed and built the house themselves, a task that took three years. But, Wally says, it was "ten years in the thinking." Inside, the house is warm and comfortable, featuring thick plank doors from old homesteads and a rock fireplace with a huge hearthstone donated by a neighbor. The cedar living room is lined with books on a wide range of subjects, evidence that Wally is also a bibliophile. The McRaes don't own a TV.

Their house isn't far from the one-room schoolhouse where, when he was four years old, Wally recited his first poem. He remembers that it was Christmastime and the poem was English. "It had the word 'ha'penny' in it. I liked that word." This was the beginning of Wally's lifelong love of words, a love that was nurtured in his family.

"We liked poetry in our home back in the forties when my sister, Marjorie, used to cut poems out of a livestock publication and glue them to a pale blue ribbon and hang them by a straight pin in her room. We didn't know Bruce Kiskaddon from Adam's off ox, but Marjorie saved and savored his poems."

 In an effort to record the values and ways of his ranching community, Wally began writing poetry over twenty-five years ago. "I was just sitting in the house waiting for a heifer to calve, so I wrote a poem." He kept on writing, filling an old boot box with verse, until he had enough pages "to throw sixty percent away and still come out with a slim volume of what was best." *It's Just Grass and Water* was published in 1979, followed by *Up North and Down the Crick* in 1985, *Things of Intrinsic Worth* in 1989, and his latest, *Cowboy Curmudgeon and Other Poems*, in 1992.

Exemplifying "the lingo of our calling," Wally's poetry reflects the complex beliefs and customs of cowboy culture. "Our cowboy way of life is diverse. We have subcultures and nuances that mark us, brand us to where we belong. We write who we are, but we're not all the same." Many of Wally's poems, such as "Reincarnation," the best known, and most often recited, contemporary cowboy poem, are stamped with his particular brand of irony and humor. Others, like "We Never Rode the Judiths" —dedicated to Canadian cowboy singer-songwriter Ian Tyson—impart Wally's love for the Montana landscape and the value he places on friendship.

Among the finest composers of ballad-style verse, Wally stretches the limits of traditional cowboy poetry. He is a kind of fulcrum between the old and the new. A man who invites challenge, he takes on the issues facing ranchers and cowboys today—use of public lands, the impact of rural development, and the ravages of strip-mining. Just ten miles from the McRae ranch, a monstrous coal-mining operation dominates the landscape.

"The kind of poetry you write depends on where you come from, not only geographically, but philosophically. Because one of the largest strip mines in the U.S. is in my back yard, I've written poems about the effect that coal-oriented industrialization has on the cowboy culture."

Wally claims that coal development in his area has made the cowboy culture that much stronger. It has led his neighbors to reawaken to those traditional values that are being threatened, and to find they're still important. "I feel strongly about wanting our way of life to go on, our family values, our love of the land. . . . We aren't out to rip off the land. It's our home. Most ranchers feel like this. We are stewards of the land and its creatures. We are one of them."

His poems are a plea for the life that he loves, that he has inherited, and that he wants to pass on, intact.

Rod McQueary

"My poetry tries to tell the truth about my culture and my profession. The only thing ranch families can be sure of is that they are misunderstood."

Life and Times

When they ask of Life,
What will I say?
Can I describe time that swirls,
Flits with fickle castanets,
And disappears?
A shrinking, self-swallowing serpent?

Sometimes in spring
When ropes with eyes
Fly to heads and heels

The smokey celebration of
Surviving another winter
Buys the seven-way and Bud

Dusty faces crack from laughing
Bloody hands pass Copenhagen
Back and forth

No furtive glances hopefully
Caress snowless ridges
Today
The future is studiously ignored
For the intensity of
Now

Ground crew limps—unnoticed
Tomorrow's hips and rope-arm
Shoulders
Get no second
Thought

If
By God
We are a primitive
Futureless band

At least we avoid
That flatland
Urban trap
Of measuring life
With
Time

For Woody

From the snowdrifts in the canyons,
Behind the granite and the pinion
Past the trout and beaver,
Where young quakies crowd, to share;
From the icy plaster caked
Across the mountain goat's dominion,
Comes the lifeblood of our valley,
As it tumbles down from there.

And it gurgles, almost chuckles
Past the boulders and the gravel.
Cheerfully, it detours
Through the ditches man might make.
With only gravity its master,
It always knows which way to travel;
Warm and foamy, ever downward,
Through the sloughs toward the lake.

There, the bullrush stops the ripples,
Where the sheets of ice lay dying.
The waxing sun shows promise
That the winter's lost its sting.
Overhead, the floating regiments
Of geese formations, flying,
Driven northward to their nesting grounds,
By instinct, every spring.

In one pasture by the water,
Tired pension horses wander.
They wait for my alfalfa,
And the sun to conquer cold.
In this middle ground, 'tween
Active duty and the promised yonder,
They don't care too much for scenery;
They are thin, and tired, and old.

Last among these pensioners,
One sorrel gelding stumbles.
With swollen knees and seedy toe,
You see why he's so lame.
He's lost his youth, but not his dignity.
He would die before he humbles.
He was my dad's top saddle horse,
And Woody is his name.

I never cared for Woody,
He's not the kind of horse I cling to.
He was hard to catch, and fussy,
And he never made a pet.
But he would jump at cattle,
That was the one thing he could do;
And he had the heart of giants,
I can still recall it yet.

We were bringing calvy heifers
From a close and handy pasture,
Bus rode bronco Woody,
'Cause he had a lot to learn.
One heifer broke, they ran to head her,
Stood their ground, and stopped disaster.
With dewclaws cutting circles,
They beat that cow at every turn. . . .

So she ran blind for the willows;
Bus and Woody had to race her,
Nose to nose, and pushing shoulders,
As she made this frantic try.
And they pushed her in a circle,
Till she quit, and they could face her.
Because Buster wouldn't weaken,
And Woody did not let her by.

And now, I watch him strain to shuffle.
I touch my rifle, 'neath the seat—
A friend to suffering horses.
At this range, I could not miss.

He'd find green pastures in an instant.
For my dad, I'd do it neat.
He'd never hear the whisper.
Never feel the Nosler's kiss.

But the cranes have come. They're dancing,
As the spring sun melts the snow.
Oh, I know I'll need that rifle
On some cold November day.
But for a sorrel colt who beat
That wringy heifer, long ago,
I'll just go about my business,
Till this feeling—goes away.

For Souls

Perhaps, he said, it's not a man's heart or mind
That drives him down to surging sea,
To straining mast.
Not mind, he said, that makes him fill
Some quivering stirrup . . . eagerly,
To float across the grunting, pounding range,
Hat fanning reckless, loose and fast.
Not mind that sends him high,
Beyond the tether of wind, or cloud;
Spear through the air to ride the sky,
Ascend the stairs, forsake the sod,
To loose the reins and challenge, proud;
Or taste the salty tears of God.

Perhaps it's not the heart, or mind,
That spurs us on from thrill to thrill,
But fluttering soul, stretching, straining,
Caged by ribs and blood, but still,
Impatiently, but uncomplaining,
It waits for some escape to find.
Beneath some struggling bronco's death,
In some tortured metal fuselage,
Or sinking calm 'neath raging wave,
Past the pain, and fear, and breath
We learn how new-freed souls behave.
Released now by this mortal's death,
Unconfined by time and space,
Brighter, lighter, upward cast,
Newborn, it wakes in some chromed tunnel
Just beyond Medusa's face
And wonders why—It's free, at last.
Great God almighty, free
    . . . at last.

For Life

If life were just one April day
And I should wake, mid-afternoon,
To feel the sunshine on my shirt,
Warm scattered raindrops wet my cheek,
I'd marvel with my newborn eyes
At the beauty I had never seen.

If life should be one April day,
I'll not pine for a morning lost
Nor mourn some teenage innocence.

But hand in hand, my love and I
Will lift one cup for fallen friends
Then, our business done,
We'll laugh till wrinkles frame our eyes.

And in these final precious hours
We'll celebrate the eveningtime.

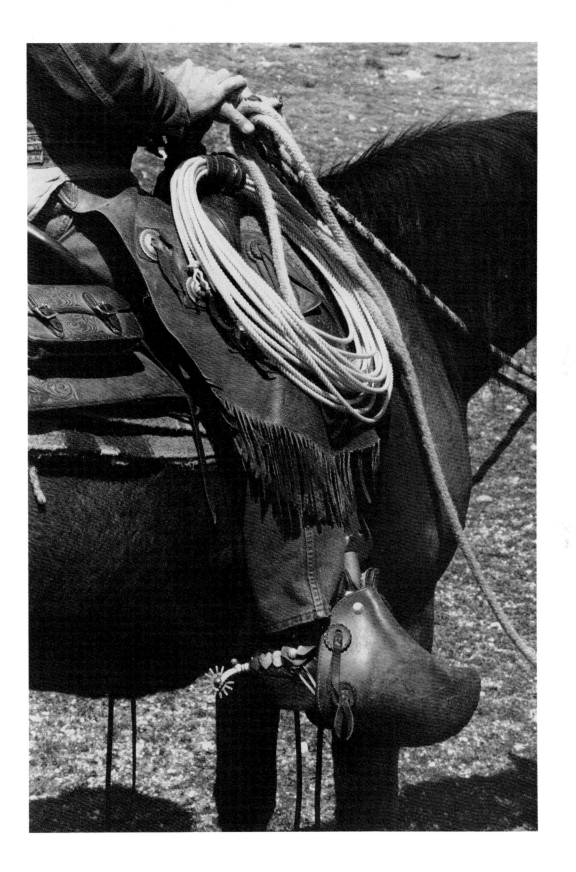

Rod McQueary's grandfather came from Colorado to Ruby Valley in 1946 and bought 3,800 deeded acres that until recently have supported 350 mother cows. Born in 1951, Rod has spent his entire life, except for a stint in the Marines, working on the UX Livestock Ranch, which lies in a remote corner of northern Nevada, eighty miles southeast of Elko and just beyond Secret Pass.

Kent and I first visited Rod in early February, after the Cowboy Poetry Gathering in Elko. The approach to Rod's ranch is a fifteen-mile stretch of dirt road. Lined with six-foot snowdrifts, the road required a four-wheel drive vehicle. The silent, white expanse of the valley Rod calls "the Lady" was broken only by cloud drifts settling over the mountain peaks. A horse skull set on a pole marked the McQueary driveway. Recently divorced, Rod made his home in a small trailer surrounded by hay bales and set into the hillside above the road. An old yellow pickup showing signs of wear was parked outside. In the truck bed was the disheveled, icy carcass of a porcupine. Later, with his deadpan delivery, Rod explained, "Al's quiet, and he doesn't criticize my driving."

Rod is a slightly built man with intense ice-blue eyes that greet visitors with a steady but friendly gaze. It has been said of Rod that everyone who meets him feels like his best friend. However, though he makes others laugh—he's given to telling wry jokes and pulling pranks on friends—he doesn't smile much. A Vietnam veteran, for over twenty years Rod was tormented by nightmares and agonizing memories. Writing poetry has played a vital part in his healing. "If I hadn't been able to write poems," he offered matter-of-factly, "I would've taken some Rompin [a large-animal tranquilizer], climbed on this rank horse I had and headed for the hills."

In a departure from "cowboy" verse, Rod collaborated with fellow vet Bill Jones on *Blood Trails*, published in 1992 by Dry Crik Press. Through poetry that is raw, powerful, and intensely personal, the authors recount their journey of liberation from the trauma of Vietnam. When someone asked how long it took him to write the poems in *Blood Trails*, which include "For Souls" and "For Life," Rod answered, "Twenty-three years." He hopes that the book will help other vets. "If we can save one life, it'll be worth a lot." To this end, Rod and Bill have given recitations, and given away copies of their book, throughout the West. All proceeds from the book go to veterans.

Rod began writing poems as a teenager at Elko High School, using humor to ward off his shyness. He calls his early pieces "my disposable poems."

But he continued writing, working to develop his own style of poetry. Many of his poems first appeared in *Dry Crik Review* and his work has since been included in a number of anthologies.

The first time Rod recited before a large audience was at the 1986 Cowboy Poetry Gathering in Elko. He knew only one poem by heart, his own "Joker's Pay," about "the sorry state of the ranching business." Despite his nervousness, Rod's recitation was an instant hit and, to his surprise, his poem was published in the program that year and also appeared in *USA Today*. Rod decided to hone his natural gift as a performer. Wearing his signature silver-belly hat, he is now one of the most sought after and accomplished presenters at Elko and other cowboy poetry gatherings. His bone-dry wit and unique minimalist delivery have made Rod popular with audiences who are now becoming aware of his skill at writing serious, deeply affecting poetry. Paul Zarzyski claims that Rod will continue to write good poems long after the phenomenon of "performance" cowboy poetry has passed. Paul says, "McQueary writes because he *needs* to write." When I told this to Rod, he quipped, "Paul meant to say, 'Rod writes because he *hates* to work.' "

Each summer, Rod has turned packer, leading groups of hunters and wilderness enthusiasts into the Ruby Mountains. On our last visit, Kent and I accompanied Rod horseback up through the sagebrush hills of Short Canyon, behind the ranch. Rod had a mission: to retrieve a small woodstove left behind by hunters years before. With the morning sun at our backs, we rode up a winding trail along a creek, stopping often to rest the horses. Rod spoke in low, reassuring tones to the pack horse and to his mount, a spirited bay gelding he bought for $1.00 from his longtime friend the cowboy poet Waddie Mitchell. They agreed that when Waddie owned his own ranch someday, he could buy the horse back—for $2.00.

There was a bittersweet quality to the trip, as Rod had made plans to sell of his cattle and take a hiatus from ranching, cowboying, and packing. That bright spring day would likely be the last time he would ride a horse up the canyon. "This could be a sad day," he told us, "but I know I'm doing the right thing."

In May of 1993, soon after our visit, Rod hit the road for new places and adventures. Before departing, during a small gathering at the White Horse Inn in Three Rivers, California, he offered these thoughts as an introduction to his poem "Life and Times": "There is an underlying tone in the ranching business these days of grief. There have been 14 million people in my lifetime go off ranches and farms and go to the city. One percent of the population of the United States left ranches and farms between 1979 and '89. With the seven-year drought that is, God help us, finally over, we hope this trend will be reversed. Maybe times will get better for us all . . ."

In October 1993 Rod cut a trail to the National Storytelling Festival in Jonesborough, Tennessee, where he says he "held his own" with the best storytellers in the country. They've invited him back next year. He's currently collaborating with Waddie Mitchell on a book, *Cowboy Stories*; and he's planning another book, *Soldier's Heart*, a collection of stories told by Vietnam vets about their lives since the war.

On July 23, 1994 Rod married Sue Wallis, his friend for many years, in a small ceremony at the County Courthouse in Elko, Nevada. His friends report that Rod is smiling more these days.

Linda Hussa

"There is a core in cowboy poetry, twisted strong like rawhide,
and that is love of the land. Above all, that.
All life centers around the land."

The Blue Filly

She is just three.
Weaned again.

First time from her dead mother
        small blue head
        in the flank of a still heart.

Second time from a spotted burro
        who let her stand near
        as they swept flies in their head-tail sleep.

Last from the mare band
        that taught her with stinging nips
        to stand back and wait.

She sees him coming.
        Hay poking out in mid-chew
        does she wonder, "What now?"

He speaks her name
        in sound and breath
        she will come to know as her own.

A halter slips over her nose
        and she follows him into the barn
        shivering.

Hobbles hold her
        while the brush sweeps
        firm and soft over her skin.

And when his hand slides down her neck
        I feel it on mine.
        We both relax
        and prepare ourselves for the sadding.

In This Moment

I felt the blow
  somewhere inside that is heart and chest
  being and feeling
  and knowing

  knowing

  the sound
  the jerk that came together.

My mare danced on four legs.
  She could not move on three.

Hoof held dangling
  muscles cramping
  eyes that clouded
  as mine closed
  on this moment laid hard against
  one so clear.

The walk away
  for the rifle
  thirty aught six
  aught—ought—ought not.

I hold the mechanics of shiny brass
  and rifling true
  the breech
  the bolt.

Marksmanship is wasted
  when the barrel fits the ear

  and she is blown
  into my memory
  where she will dance.

A Birth

Across the ditch
     she turns and stands
     as pain rolls down her side
     tail cast
     her nose drags the blur of snow and mud
     ignoring cows feeding past, calves stretched sleeping.

I try not to intrude.
     Some things are better left to reach their own point of
     brilliance
     even if they involve pain.

But there is a tension
     a line deepening below her eye.
There is a tightness
     in the twist of her lip.
Even from this distance I can read
     the silence in her eyes.

Once in the barn and tied
I seek to right the thing gone awry.

Crimson scarves blow and swirl around my arm
     —the heat surprising—
     my fingers gently probe a sacred place.
Feet curled back
     the calf she wants to bear is blocked.
I work between her pressing
     pushing back to give room
     to draw the legs forward, one at a time.
Her body stiffens
     her eyes look beyond the present
     to a place of pain she has no reckoning of.
     Moments locked down on her.

I clear the feet, then the pasterns
a tip of black tongue curls
licks my arm.
I sit down behind her
brace my feet against her trembling legs
we have a tug of war with this calf.
Her great groan is duet with mine.
There runs a red beading tear,
a crunching give,
and birth.

Under the Hunter Moon

I slip the rifle sling over my shoulder
    and step into the silence of dawn.
Geese move through the darkened sky
    toward the pond.
      Wings cut the quiet
      with an oddly mechanical sound
      and their voices set me right.

I open the gate.
The sheep rise from their beds
    as if I commanded it so.
Lambs rush to thump flanks for milk
    kept warm through the autumn night.

I fall in with their march up the meadow
    to find clover that grew while they slept.
Stalks of blue chicory and tiny golden trefoil
    fold inside pink lips, and chewing,
    they walk on.

At the fence line I know the place
    where soft pads left prints in the dust
    by a hole in the woven wire
    and I am a warrior hunched in rose briars
    their scent pale, and their thorns pick at my wool coat.

Stern in my resolve
    I wait while the sun creeps to the edge of the day.
Slain lambs, guts ripped open.
Magpies and blow flies.
Bleating ewes with swollen bags searching the flock.

A lamb a day for two weeks.
    I grip the rifle tighter.

A shadow comes toward me through the moonlight
    gray and tan, she arches in a mouse pounce
    and works her way toward the barrel of my rifle,
    toward the bullet I will hurl
    at her heart.

I watch her snatch mice out of the grass
    flip them up like popcorn,
    down the hatch. She is a comic
    this coyote, playing, laughing
    making her way steadily toward me
    my finger soft on the cold steel trigger.

Coyote stops
    looks directly at me.
Her eyes hold me accountable.

The Hussa Ranch lies at the end of a long road in what is known as the "sagebrush corner" of northeastern California. Surprise Valley, named by settlers who passed through on the Emigrant Trail to California and Oregon, has been a ranching community for over a hundred years. To the west the Warner Mountains soar up from the valley floor, sheltering this place from the outside world. To the east lies the "American outback"—the wild and remote high desert of the Great Basin. The small town of Cedarville is less than two miles from the ranch. There are no stoplights in town, but there is a drugstore with an old-fashioned soda fountain.

Linda Hussa moved to Surprise Valley over twenty years ago, when she married John, a third-generation rancher. "My life began when I came to Surprise Valley," she says. The Hussas live in the comfortable two-story ranch house in which John grew up, surrounded by towering poplars and cottonwoods. The trees provide shade from the hot summer sun for three dogs and more than a dozen cats. Besides running a cow-calf operation, John and Linda raise and train ranch horses. In recent years they've gotten into the sheep business as well. Linda says with a laugh, "I thought I was a buckaroo but during lambing I turn into a mutton buster."

John and Linda, along with John's father, Walter, rise at four A.M. to a workday that often lasts until dark, tending and doctoring their animals, haying, assisting at the birth—and sometimes witnessing the death—of lambs and calves. It is a life lived close to the marrow of existence. Linda claims that hard work is what cements the values of ranch life. "You do the work till the work gets done. The work itself is the thing."

Born in eastern Oregon, Linda is the daughter of the well-known Arabian-horse training partners, Lee and Bette Vinson. Her parents shared a passion for horses that runs strong through three generations. Following their lead, Linda competed in stock-horse and cutting competitions. When her father took a job training for John Rogers Arabian Ranch, the family moved to Walnut Creek, California, near San Francisco. Linda went to highschool in Danville, followed by two years at Diablo Valley College in Pleasant Hill. She says she never really adapted to suburban living.

Things changed when she moved to Surprise Valley. Ranch life seemed to be what she was suited for. "In ranching, horses are the means.

I found a new way of riding. I'd never roped before. John was a patient teacher. He helped me learn to cowboy up—to be a buckaroo instead of just a rider." In those early days, the Hussa Ranch shared a 300-square-mile grazing permit with two other ranches, forming the Alkali Cattle Company. Linda was the only woman buckaroo in the outfit. Here is how she describes her role:

"During the fall gather, the company was split into two groups: the circle crew and the shippers. The shippers stayed in camp, ate a hot lunch, and took a nap. We were the riders. We sat on our own side of the table. We took no lunch and we covered the country in ten days or two weeks. We trotted. Sometimes all day. We each had a string of four or five horses, so they had a couple of rest days between the rides. Those horses covered a lot of country."

Linda bristles when anyone assumes that a woman can't buckaroo as well as a man. Her soft-spoken, gentle demeanor and ready sense of humor are partnered with a quiet strength, an unquestioning sense of her own capabilities. When I arrived for a two-day visit, she told me I'd missed out on the fun—the day before, she'd roped a coyote down by the lake. All part of a day's work.

No less impressive than Linda's prowess horseback are her gifts as an artist—her delicately hued watercolors adorn the walls of the ranch house—and as a writer. She has written articles, short stories, and a book, *Diary of a Cow Camp Cook*, her chronicle of a modern-day cattle drive. Several years ago, she began writing poetry, now her chosen form of expression. Her work is included in several anthologies and a collection of her poems, *Where the Wind Lives*, was published in 1994. In April 1994, Linda was invited, along with Paul Zarzyski and Sonny Hancock, to give a reading at the Library of Congress in Washington, D.C. Inherent in Linda's poetry is a reverence for life and a strong sense of place. "This place, this way of life, is *the* ingredient of my writing."

Linda credits John with instilling in her a deep respect for the pioneer families of their "sagebrush corner." As a past president and long time member of the Modoc County Historical Society, Linda worked on the oral history program, capturing on videotape the oldtimers' stories of the people who struggled to live in Surprise Valley, which was settled in the mid-1860s. "Doing the oral histories taught me about these people, who they were, how they lived their lives. I want to tell these stories."

Through poetry, Linda reaches down to those stories, into her own life and other peoples' lives, finding those things that touch her. She wants to let others know that ranching people live a life that has value.

"The loss of community in this country and the need to connect is very real . . . We as poets are separated, isolated, yet we come together as if our lives were spent a ridge away. We are rooted and we do belong. We care about our neighbors. That is what draws people to cowboy poetry. And it takes a poet to tell about the living with purpose, with honor. It is our place, our pride, to do the telling."

John Dofflemyer

"Ranching culture may hold the tools for the survival of the whole—
the thought processes which underscore man's relationship
with the land in terms more congruent with natural truth."

Upstream

Sunrise sorts the shadowed shapes
through cobwebbed windows,
new tracks of dreams
left dancing on old wallpaper
I cannot read
awake.

I run upstream through time,
a bouldered creek thick
with alders and dogwood bloom
offering no bank escape—
thigh weary and wet
I float back
as daylight empties
into a wider river
  flats and farms
  consumed by cities below.

The channel to the sea is lost—
no way back
  to the granite lakes
  where cumulus float
  on blue
  where I once walked
  on the edge
  of clouds.

When the Redbuds Come

The raw redbud time colors
the mountain cowboy dance
beyond all metaphors of worry.

The brush-busting high-lope
of supple leather blooms
with wide-loop wings
singing now
singing scarlet with the instant
sign reborn from generations
of beast & man.
The last tribe of "yahoos"
to loan their souls to eagles
without a penny in their pants.

When sweat cakes horseflesh
grazing saddleless in sweet feed,
     the crunching murmur joins
     the deafening buzz
     of springing
without words.
In unison we watch
the disappearing moment
we have become.

The Sierra's Spine

The new moon smeared
with autumn clouds
I allow as harbingers
for a wet winter—
the Sierras between us again

& if I were truly romantic
I'd roach the mules
saddle an extra horse
ride three days
from Cedar Grove
& bring you home
the long way

instead I imagine
how this yellow crescent hangs
above the steep east wall
of granite and tailings

your mother
& two sisters camped
for the week
on Rock Creek
as you scatter
your father.

Chagoopa Plateau

for W. E. DeCarteret

Where the pine twists short with knotted
Roots below bare Mt. Kaweah,
Flow eroded sandy deserts
Linked in landscapes with the moon,
Where the snow and shade have squatted
Strung in meadows on Chagoopa,
Angels strum in quiet concert
To the wild chords sung in tune.

Beneath the dome atop this planet
Stretchin blue and pure and trackless
Intrudes the tame in quivers
And the wild still stare in awe
In the shavins carved from granite
Where the winter's work is timeless
Well above the busy rivers
Years a cuttin natural law.

It is here in God's own parlor
With no evil dare trespassin
Where a sinner gets religion
And a preacher'd kneel & pray
That a young man hears the clapper
Of the bell mare he is huntin:
Just regular imagination
Like some church too far away.

Should he leave the tracks he's followed
From the beaver dams and meadows
Where the Kern has slowed its cuttin
Down through miles of broken rock
To pursue the sound that's echoed
In his brain with innuendoes
Now that he's this close to heaven
On Chagoopa searchin stock?

But the clapper rings too steady
To be mare and horses grazin,
No natural gong he knows is real,
But it tempts him just the same
In the air sucked thin to heady
Thoughts that keep a young man brazen
With dreams afloat well off the trail
That's now become too tame.

It's the magic of Chagoopa
Clear above the world of humans
Where young men huntin horses
Learn the most about the wild
Just below bare Mt. Kaweah
Tumbles real & those illusions
Mixin free with mystic forces
Carvin men out of a child.

Like his father and grandfather before him, John Dofflemyer runs a cow-calf operation at the confluence of the Kaweah River and Dry Creek, east of Visalia, California, in the foothills of the Sierra Nevada below Sequoia National Park. His mother's great-grandfather, John Cutler, was Tulare County's first judge and doctor, involved in the cattle business and early politics. Cutler also wrote verses about his travels through the then mostly uninhabited San Joaquin Valley.

Born in 1948, John graduated from the Webb School of California in 1966 and earned a B.S. degree at the University of Southern California in Los Angeles, after which he returned home to pursue what he calls a "less lucrative but rewarding lifestyle." It was in urban Southern California twenty-five years ago that John began to write poems. Much of what he wrote about was the place and the life he'd left behind. "Our sense of place is our environment . . . When I was livin' in L.A., I'd come back here to get sane."

A visit to Dry Creek Ranch, located in a remote canyon several miles north of the small town of Lemon Cove, is like stepping back in time. Reminiscent of early California ranchland, this range and riparian area is registered with the Nature Conservancy. It is home to plentiful and diverse species of wildlife: mule deer, feral pigs (John says of these creatures that are favorite targets for hunters, "I leave 'em alone; they're revertin' back to the wild"), cougar, and osprey, the white "sea eagle" which roosts in the tall sycamores along Dry Creek. There is abundant archeological evidence of the area's first inhabitants, the Yokuts, on this and surrounding ranches. The site of an Indian village and Creation center, along with countless petroglyphs, now lie underwater, lost beneath the lake created by Terminus Dam.

On a cool April afternoon Kent and I walked with John through knee-high spring grass near the banks of Dry Creek. "I grew up catchin' bullfrogs in this crick," he said. He paused and looked off. "This is my life."

For years, John recalled, "I didn't have it lined out what I wanted in life. I tried working, tried hard. All the formulas didn't work." Then in 1989 a friend asked him to come to the Cowboy Poetry Gathering in Elko. Going to the event was, he said, "just a lark," but it changed his life. "For me, Elko embodied an atmosphere of caring and acceptance—it is changing, yet that thread is still there among all of us who connect there."

John notes that the deep emotions that are part of the scene at Elko are mostly conveyed not in words, but by a kind of body language, certain gestures peculiar to tight-lipped cowboys. His own participation in the Gatherings, he says, "balanced out that tough guy I'd been tryin' to be."

Just over the hill from the creek, less than a mile from the log house John is building, a large gravel pit gouges the gently rolling canyonland. To make way for this marginal operation, ten percent of one of the largest inland stands of western sycamores in the state was leveled, along with valley oaks four to five centuries old. This senseless destruction of trees that were part of John's childhood landscape was for him a profound emotional loss. With stubborn determination, fueled by his love for the land, John wages a maverick's lonely battle against this kind of encroachment.

"The landscape is our memory. It holds the memory for us. Once you change the landscape, you not only lose personal memory, you lose that sense of tradition." He fears that if we continue to change the landscape, we're going to lose our whole culture and tradition.

In an attempt "to capture the notions and values that are intrinsic to this culture," and as a way to provide a written balance to the oral tradition of cowboy poetry, in 1991 John published the first issue of *Dry Crik Review*. Known for expanding the limits of cowboy poetry—the Vietnam poems of Rod McQueary and Bill Jones were first published in *Dry Crik Review*—and for presenting the strongest new voices in this rapidly expanding movement, including a growing number of women, *Dry Crik Review* is a maverick among literary publications. It reflects John's faith in the individual voice of every poet he publishes.

John's own poetry is no less confined by tradition. In a style that he says "vacillates with the muses," he depicts the life and conflicts facing cowmen today, particularly the increasing threat of urban growth and development. His pastoral poems reflect his deep respect for, and sense of oneness with, what he calls Mother Nature. They are a reflection of one man's relationship with his setting, including the people and the atmosphere in which he pursues his livelihood.

John has published several chapbooks: *Dry Creek Rymes* and *Sensin' Somethin'*," in 1989, followed in 1990 by *Black Mercedes*, and then *Muses of the Ranges* in 1991, *Hung Out to Dry* in 1992, and *Cattails* in 1993. He has also edited an anthology of cowboy poetry, *Maverick Western Verse*. Despite the demands of ranching and tending livestock, he continues to publish quarterly issues of *Dry Crik Review*. In the introduction to a recent issue, John wrote, "I think we're making history here, but I'm also susceptible to dreams."

Part of John's dream, and possibly his biggest challenge, is to bridge the chasm between urban and rural worlds, "to communicate the worth of those in the range livestock culture to a majority that doesn't understand us beyond a nostalgic or Hollywood past or a media-hyped present." Instead, he invites a broader understanding that "we're all human." And John hopes that in his and others' poems "the voice of the land can be heard well enough that we may all learn to listen more closely."

Shadd Piehl

"I'm not tryin' to get to deep truths. I'm just tellin' stories."

Storm Front

1.

The colt noses the water,
Paws, muddies the creek.
At my insistence he gathers
And crosses in a great lunge.
I hunt leather as we crash
Over tangles of buffalo brush,
Leaving the draw in crow-hop leaps.
I am glad we are alone, and unseen.

2.

On top, gray clouds the sun,
Trails smokey veils of rain.
The wind picks up mane, jumps
Through grass, sings dust.
As I pull down my hat, the dun
Raises his head and cries to horses
On dark hills. Along the storm front
A red-tail hawk hangs still.

3.

I chuck us into a slow lope,
Then into a cold falling wall.
Letting the colt have his head,
I hide mine beneath hat brim, in
A fool's trust of a three-year-old.
The world becomes one of sound
And touch, between myself and earth
The running horse. Thunder

4.

Explodes beneath the mist;
I watch grass blur past.
Listen—The day single-foots
As we run. Somewhere the hawk
Waits it out in a tree. The horses

Have their asses to the wind.
This rain that wets us is the same
That runs to the creek, and chills
The hawk, horses and hills.

5.
After rolling in the corral,
Does the muddled colt forget
Our run—far horses, red hawk
And dark storm? I, again the fool,
Wonder. Was our ride the rain?
Is the creek our lives?
The braided hair rope, my mecate,
Is rough and stiffens in my hands.

Whether drifting through life on a boat or climbing toward old age leading a horse, each day is a journey and the journey itself is home.

—Bashō

My Grandfather's and Father's Horses

The two old-timers stand out west of town
With maybe a few cows to share
A bale and ground feed each morning.
King, over thirty, is swaybacked, slow
And still impossible to catch
(except by tricks, women and oats).
Cheese, once a terror in the corral,
Now no longer rules the roost.
In their old age they shy,
Meeting themselves in shadows
At the water trough.
Both needing their teeth floated,
Dun horses out to pasture.
Every cowboy has a horse that's not for sale.

Winter Breaks

A mist hangs sentient in the hills
We lope through, checking cow
Calf pairs along a creek swollen
Yellow with sunken ice and leaves.
The spray freezes, collects white
In the sorrel's mane and drums
In wild rhythms off my hat.

We are driven across the sky
By hail, until blocked on a bench
By a slender black and white
Growth of poplar. Winter, its
Remains heavy-grained banks,
Slowly melts into runoff
Descends the grouse-colored folds.

My pony, slipping and scrabbling
Down a bank, balks at the dark
Smells of an oak-vaulted cut, or
The muted cadence of released water.
A white jackrabbit, ears tipped black,
Springs from the snow, and the colt
Snorts in panic, ducks back, slips

Goes down rolling on thawing earth.
Falling clear, I struggle in mud to
Hang to the reins. My white-eyed
Bronc breaks free; left kneeling in the run,
I bow and drink the cold flow of buffalo
Grass. Turning, I follow the rhythmic
Spate, beginning my own journey home.

Towards Horses

for Tom Mau and Kenny Taton

"Bronc stompers, hell roarers
And all-around hands, going to the peelin'."

Near Castle Butte, the clouds
Hang in wavy mare's-tails,
Appaloosa thin and carded
Against a sky with too little blue.
The plain's irrigated hay land
Has been made into round bales
That roll with us to Rapid City.
Tom is reading the *Sports News*.
Kenny wakes and shuffles cards
For another round of pitch.
I set the cruise at seventy-five,
And we play, past the Belle Fourche,
Past Bear Butte, weaving between
Black Hills tourist Winnebagos.
The air cools and becomes as charged
As they who travel towards horses,
Living the days by tokens:
Horses.   Creek.
                              Sky.
        Bronc saddles.   Butte.
Never ending road.

Shadd Piehl was raised outside Minot, North Dakota, along the breaks of the Mouse River. "That land is home to me. I s'pose that's where that feel for the land comes from in my poetry." There is a deep-felt regard for place in all of Shadd's poems, along with a love of isolation engendered by the endless, rolling plains. Many North Dakotans leave, trading the relentless wind, the bitter cold of winter, and the remoteness of their state for the prospect of an easier life elsewhere. Not one to follow the crowd, Shadd is determined to remain. "I think it's better for my poetry if I stay in one place," he explains in a softly clipped Midwestern accent.

Born in Dickinson, North Dakota, in 1967, Shadd moved to Minot in 1972 when his father, Walter, a well-known western artist, got a job teaching art at Minot State University. Walter was also a well-known bronc rider and rodeo announcer, and Shadd's grandfather, Walter Piehl, Sr., was a rodeo stock contractor. "I was always around rodeo," Shadd says. "My first words were, 'Buck 'em.' " Almost before he could walk, Shadd was riding roping calves, then he graduated to Shetland ponies and "anything they put me on." It wasn't long before he tried calf roping and team roping, followed by bull and bareback bronc riding. But he always wanted to ride saddle broncs. "Saddle-bronc riding grew out of cowboyin', gettin' on those bad horses, those bad buckers. I figured if you're going to rodeo, that's the closest to the real thing. It's the classic event of rodeo."

In late August, Kent and I met up with Shadd and his brother, Levi, at a night rodeo in Billings, Montana. Hank Real Bird was there too, guiding his sons as they competed in saddle-bronc riding. I was struck by Shadd's intensity as he went about his preparations behind the bucking chute. Before he lowered himself onto the back of a white-eyed bronc, he slapped each side of his face, hard.

Describing the allure of bronc riding, Shadd told me, "I guess you've gotta be kind of a thrill seeker. When you get on a good buckin' horse who's really givin' it his all and you can ride him well for eight seconds, that's all there is in the world." However, Shadd's dream of making a living out of rodeo faded after two knee surgeries and a broken back, which he suffered when a horse fell over backwards on him. "My body may not allow me to do this much longer. Rocky Kubla—a veteran bronc rider who taught me a lot—says that by the time you learn how to ride broncs you're too beat up or too broke up to do it."

It was his interest in rodeo that led Shadd to North Dakota State University in Fargo, which had one of the best college rodeo teams in the state. It wasn't long before Shadd became a two-time winner of the Great Plains Region Intercollegiate Championships, and he won an amateur state title as well. Besides competing in his favorite sport, Shadd majored in journalism and became an editor of the school paper. In his junior year, soon after he'd decided he wanted to pursue a career as an English teacher, he came across "a real good instructor and a good poet," David Martinson. Martinson introduced Shadd to the world of poetry and he soon began writing poems. "I'd always thought that way, but up until then, I didn't know what to do with those lines in my head."

While he was still in college, Shadd sent some of his poems to John Dofflemyer, who published them in *Dry Crik Review*. John suggested that Shadd send a tape of his work to the Western Folklife Center in Elko, Nevada. In 1993 Shadd was invited to participate in Elko's annual Cowboy Poetry Gathering. It was the first time he'd ever been on a plane. He says he was "blown away" by the experience, especially by the warm response from appreciative audiences. However, he admits that he's not entirely comfortable with such attention.

A strong new voice in the contemporary cowboy poetry movement, Shadd says he gets many of his ideas for poems "goin' down the road" to rodeos. Yet, so far, he hasn't written much about the actual experience of bronc riding—maybe, he thinks, because he's too close to it. Speaking of poetry, he says, "I like the language, the sound of words." The language and the words come to him in images, which he attributes to growing up with an artist father. Shadd is an admirer of fellow Dakotan Thomas McGrath, as well as Ezra Pound—he once carved a line from a Pound poem into his saddle—Kenneth Rexroth, and Bashō, the seventeenth-century Japanese haiku master. All, he says, have influenced his poetry.

The distinct Indian spirit in Shadd's poetry undoubtedly derives in part from the land itself, as North Dakota is Indian country. Shadd also acknowledges the influence of his younger sisters, Crystal and Dahcota, who are Lakota. Shadd's parents adopted the girls when non-Indians could still legally adopt Indian children. While Shadd and his brother and sisters were growing up, their parents would often read them Indian myths, and Shadd remembers that the few books of poetry in the house were Native American.

In the fall of 1993, Shadd began teaching high school English on the Turtle Mountain Indian Reservation at Belcourt, North Dakota, ten miles from the Canadian border. Turtle Mountain, home of the Chippewas, already has an uncommon literary precedent, as it is the reservation on which author Louise Erdrich was raised.

Before he left for the "rez," Shadd told me he was looking forward to the isolation, to being able to lock himself in a room and write poems. And when spring comes, he'll probably hit the rodeo trail again, riding saddle broncs. "People tell me I should stop, but it's a tough deal to quit. There's somethin' about winning that doesn't last forever . . ."

Paul Zarzyski

"I'm ridin' that poem in my mind before I put the first spur-lick on the page . . . If the words and images and sentiments ring true, it's very much akin to making a classy ride on a snappy bronc."

Staircase

For Joe Podgurski

How can lovers of buckers lament
a favorite bronc down
and dying on timberline range
we glass for elk—meadow
he's pawed to a raw circle
around him like mool. What can we say
under this scant angle of Montana
half-moon, when we wish the whole
universe would grieve
for one rodeo star, throwing all
his heart into each roll
and futile lunge for all fours—
first stand he learned
as a colt, gravity back then pulling less
against him.
                    Like two helpless sailors
marooned with age, and mourning
a familiar orca beached
in the storm's debris, we crutch
our feeble human frames
beneath the horse's weight and heave
each time he tries. The Rockies return
our holler in a salvo of shouts,
grandstand uproar
we hope will spring him
to his feet. We pack in water, last-meal
grain and pellets. No way can we swallow easy
looking into the white of a single eye
sinking, giving in to red. No way
hunters can repent—can we take back the metal,
aimed or stray, sent through flesh.

Riflefire

across this big-game state
echoes reports of 44 wars
from guerrilla worlds, the unarmed falling
fair prey as varmint, as target,
when killing comes
nonchalant. What's one shot more—mercy
or otherwise—one more animal soul
to this planetful of procreating shots
and souls?
          Yearlings gallop a kettledrum
roll along the rim. What I can say
in light of this violent world, I hold
silent: Staircase, number 12,
bucker who broke my partner's neck in '78,
who flung me off 3 times
to hometown fans, I wanted this
life of ours—love for what hurt us most—
to last a full, eternal, 8 seconds more.

Words Growing Wild in the Woods

A boy thrilled with his first horse,
I climbed aboard my father hunkering in hip boots
below the graveled road berm, Cominski Crick
funneling to a rusty culvert. Hooking
an arm behind one of my knees, he lifted
with a grunt and laugh, his creel harness creaking,
splitshot clattering in our bait boxes.

I dreamed a Robin Hood-Paladin-Sinbad life
from those shoulders. His jugular pulse rumbled
into the riffle of my pulse, my thin wrists
against his Adam's apple—a whiskered knuckle
prickly as cucumbers in our garden
where I picked night crawlers, wet and moonlit,
glistening between vines across the black soil.

Eye-level with an array of flies, every crayon
color fastened to the silk band
of his tattered fedora, the hat my mother vowed
a thousand times to burn, I learned to love
the sound of words in the woods—Jock Scott,
Silver Doctor, Mickey Finn, Quill Gordon, Gray
Ghost booming in his voice through the spruce.

At five, my life rhymed with first flights
bursting into birdsong. I loved
the piquant smell of fiddleheads and trilliums,
hickory and maple leaf humus, the petite
bouquets of arbutus we picked for Mom.
I loved the power of my father's stride
thigh-deep against the surge of dark swirls.

Perched offshore on a boulder—safe from wanderlust
but not from currents coiling below—
I prayed to the apostles for a ten-pounder
to test the steel of my telescopic pole,
while Dad, working the water upstream and down,
stayed always in earshot—alert and calling to me
after each beaver splash between us.

I still go home to relearn my first love for words
echoing through those woods: *I caught one!*
Dad! I caught one! Dad! Dad!
skipping like thin flat stones down the crick—
and him galloping through popples, splitshot ticking,
to find me leaping for a fingerling, my first
brookie twirling from a willow like a jewel.

Luck of the Draw

For Kim and Maria Zupan, Red and Luke Shuttleworth

That holy moment I rode the bay,
Whispering Hope, this rodeo arena—
like a shrine I return to again and again,
like religion itself—was filled with bawling holler,
dust and hoofbeats. The blur of cowboy colors
shimmered brilliant as boyhood Septembers
among birch and sugar maples, where I played
decked-out like TV bronc twister,
Stoney Burke.
              But that was before
high school fans cheered us
galloping against rivals under gladiator lights
those fall Fridays in the pits, number 72
afire for 48 minutes of forearm shiver
and crack-back block.
                It's hard to believe
there was a time I forgot the roughstock
rider gutting it out
to the final gun, the whole
gridiron game's worth of physical grit
concentrated, pressed into one play,
into one 8-second ride. All I needed was a horse
and the words of Horace Greeley in a dream,
a western pen pal, a cowboy
serial flashback, some sign or cue
to make me imagine the chute gate
thrown open to the snap—cleats
and spurs, chaps and pads, high kicks,
hard hits and heartbeats synchronized
a thousand miles apart.
                I left home barely
soon enough to make one good
bucking horse ride
across a vast canvas of Russell landscape

backdropped by Heart Butte under a fuchsia sky
in Cascade, Montana.
                          Through these cottonwoods,
high above the Missouri River's silent swirls,
the flicking together of leaves
is the applause of small green hands, children
thrilled by a winning ride, by their wildest wish
beginning, as everything begins, with luck
of the draw, with a breeze in the heat,
with whispering hope—a first breath
blessed by myth, or birth, in the West.

A Song Moment for Ian Tyson

Gripping the latigo-leather straps of the black canvas
riggin' sack in his riding hand, he reaches through
the wood-beam trestle's latticework into the darkness
out over the river. It has never felt this heavy—never
felt this light. As if blackness has embraced blackness
and it has become buoyant in the black air. As if his
flexed forearm and elbow, wedged in a vee of trusses,
have petrified and grafted there.

He has finally decided to leave the arena of men behind,
to let go of his first lover, rodeo, and now he feels
suddenly like a lonely man in a world of anxious women.
The river-purl below is a woman's whisper beckoning;
the evergreens in the wind are dancehall girls in frilly
skirts and fishnet stockings; the land surrounding him
has ten thousand breasts; the night sky is a dark picture-
show aglitter with women's firefly eyes. And *she* is
locked hip to hip against him, his free arm wrapped
behind her and reaching almost all the way around—his
hand spread wide, his thumb pressed to her breastbone,
his fingers against her ribs like a blues piano-man
holding a sad last note he wishes he could hold forever,
or at least long enough to drown out the sound of a
splash. He has always feared deep water.

With one arm draped around his shoulders, she reaches
her free hand out and cups it over his fist clenching
the riggin' sack's straps. As if waiting for the opening
note to the next waltz or tango, they hold that pose
for what seems an eternity. So far they have not spoken
a word. They touch and feel their way through the intricate
steps, because they know it is the dance, not the dancers,
that matters most. As his strained arm begins to tremble,
she trembles with him. And who's to say the trestle does not
also tremble, as it did thousands of nights long ago
under the steam locomotive's lumbering, rocking gait—

bison bulls with their harems in tow. Who's to say this
couple must not hold fast until their rodeo ghosts can hop
the ghost freight passing beside them now?

Because she has been down the road herself, because she
has won and lost, and has seen him win and seen him lose,
and now, maybe, will see him walk away from roughstock
for good, she is the only woman who can know. Not only
that, but she has let other men on other bridges on other
dark nights hold on to her while they tried so hard to
let go of other boyhood dreams. She cannot help but wonder:
does the river—like a train, like a life—have its own
mysterious roundhouse way of circling back?

He breathes deeply into windy swirls of her auburn hair.
Beyond her shampoo and perfume, beyond the faint whiff
of water- and wind-worn creosote, he smells the sweet
rosin breeze through limbs of ponderosa and western fir.
She feels his fingers tighten around the straps and to her
ribs. And he feels the tempo of her heart, a snappy bronc.
"Hang on. HANG ON!", she had cheered so often to herself
as she watched him ride—the Barstowe bareback riggin',
Hank Abbie horsehide glove, and Blackwood spurs helping
him keep those hammerheads gathered beneath him for 8
seconds, now all out over the river. It is not easy for her
even to *wish* "let go." No way could she ever whisper it.

So maybe it was the full moon rising for the first time
in decades without its blue roan buckin' horse shadow. Or
maybe the wind through the trestle's framework making
the joyful sounds of the Zuni flute player. Whatever it was
that turned them loose, it was as if they'd been swept
upward like helium figurines dancing across the night
sky—the stars marking the spots where they touched down,
ever-so-lightly, with the toes of their boots.

PAUL ZARZYSKI

PAUL ZARZYSKI

Paul Zarzyski, the self-proclaimed "Polish-Hobo-Rodeo-Poet of Flat Crick, Montana," lives twenty miles outside Augusta, in the heart of Charles M. Russell country. It is a land of breathtaking grandeur—cloud shadows moving across rolling hills and deep coulees, fields dotted with round hay bales, Haystack Butte and the Front Range of the Rockies rising in the distance. Paul has said that he sees himself as "a microscopic speck in the midst of this powerful landscape that allows my presence."

The directions he gave to Kent and me indicate the remoteness of the place: "One mile past Wolf Creek, take Route 287 toward Augusta. Go twenty miles till you come to Bowman's Corner, then keep going six or seven miles, past the Hutterite Colony, turn left at the missile silo onto Flat Crick Road, go three miles, past Grammy Bean's old place, turn left at the narrow dirt crossroad, over the crick, and you'll see the cottonwoods up ahead—that's the house."

Inside, the old two-story ranch house is filled to overflowing with cowboy kitsch. Paul and his partner, folklorist Elizabeth Dear, are confessed "junking" junkies. The standouts are the cowgirl pinball machine in the living room and Paul's collection of hand-painted cowboy neckties hanging in the bedroom. On the walls are a dozen framed stop-action photos of Paul in his glory days as a bronc rider.

Above Paul's desk—and his 1952 Smith Corona typewriter (he says he'll *never* own a computer)—are photographs of his mother and father, Ernest Hemingway, E. B. White, Muhammed Ali, and Robert Penn Warren, along with William Faulkner's Nobel Prize address, a mounted jackalope head, and the Australian flag—a memento of a cowboy poetry tour of Australia a few years back.

Born in 1951, Paul grew up in Hurley, Wisconsin, an early-day logging and iron-ore mining town. Emulating his father, who worked the Cary Mine, Paul began as a boy to toil at "blue-collar, hard labor jobs." He hunted and fished with his dad, made "hard hits on the gridiron" and, when he was older, worked with livestock on Wisconsin farms. Since his youth, Paul has possessed an uncommon rapport with animals—both domestic and wild—that figures in many of his poems. At age eleven, he came West with his uncle. Montana made an indelible impression on him.

After graduating from the University of Wisconsin with degrees in biology and English, Paul went to Missoula to study poetry with Richard Hugo at the University of Montana. He received his M.F.A. in 1975. He has held teaching positions in the Forestry School and the English Department at the University of Montana. In 1981 he published his first chapbook, *Call Me Lucky*, followed by *The Make-Up of Ice* in 1984. His popular book, *Roughstock Sonnets*, published in 1989, is a collaboration with photographer Barbara Van Cleve. His work has also appeared in various anthologies, as well as in literary journals such as *Poetry*, *Elkhorn Review*, and *CutBank*.

Since his days at the University, Paul has called Montana home. At age twenty-three, he took up bronc riding and competed on both the amateur and pro rodeo circuits until a back injury terminated his career. It is a loss that has been painfully hard to live with, more so emotionally than physically, for rodeo is Paul's passion.

This love for bronc riding, and the pain of letting go, are captured in the poignant imagery of "A Song Moment for Ian Tyson." The poem led to a collaboration between Paul and Tyson on the lyrics for a song, "Rodeo Road." (The song is included on Tyson's album, *Eighteen Inches of Rain*, released by Vanguard Records in 1994.)

During a rainy-day excursion to the old Helmsville rodeo arena where Paul rode his first bronc, I asked him how his love affair with rodeo began. "The first time I was around the chutes I felt a kinship, like I'd done this before. I liked the horses, the wildness in 'em. They were renegades, and so was I." Given his intense, go-for-broke nature, it's not surprising that Paul would choose bareback bronc riding, the most physically demanding event in rodeo.

"I lived in those eight seconds more than most people do in eight years— I've never felt more *alive* than I have aboard a high-rollin' bronc. At its best, it's you and the horse doin' the dance the best it can be done." Paul says it's much the same in writing poetry. "It's just like shakin' your face for the gate, puttin' that first word on the page. Anything can happen after that, if you're letting the poem have its head."

Paul didn't always feel this way. Growing up in a "bookless house," he fell in love with words during excursions into the woods with his dad, as described in "Words Growing Wild in the Woods." But it wasn't until college that he discovered poetry which addressed experiences and emotions he could relate to. Paul credits Richard Hugo with teaching him almost everything he knows about poetry. Hugo taught him to pay as much attention to the "music" as to the "message" of a poem, and he encouraged in Paul a love of language and words that turned poetry into a "partner for life." It was Hugo who showed Paul that he could use poems to express his passion for rodeo. " 'The only rule,' Dick used to say about writing, 'is don't be boring.' That's a rule I've tried to live my life by."

Paul first heard cowboy poetry in the same room—the University's botany lecture hall—where he last heard Hugo recite. The cowboy poet was

Wallace McRae. Paul has written that McRae's poems "sent the same passionate punch to my solar plexus, that same Hugo-musical delight to my tympanum." This is the effect of Paul's own adrenaline-rush performances as a featured poet at Elko and other cowboy poetry gatherings. Paul's visceral free verse poems—"like the open range, before fences"—have expanded the traditional rhymed-verse style of cowboy poetry into a whole new arena.

A "literati" poet who has found overwhelming acceptance in the world of the "lariati," Paul has come up with his own definition of cowboy poetry: "the ring and ricochet of lingo off the stirrup-bone of the middle ear." He claims that few vernaculars lend themselves so readily, or so musically, to poetry—"because a large part of living 'the life' is living the language of 'the life.'"

Paul currently "makes a living" writing, teaching, and performing poetry. His choice in life, he says, is between time and money. He chooses time. Paul brings his passion for language, and for living to poetry workshops, where he tells his students, "Sharing emotions and ideas is what writing is all about. What life is all about."

Sue Wallis

"When I compose poetry, I try to grab words, stuff them full of who and what I am, fill them with a sense of being and place. Then I try to make them sing."

A Thousand Pretty Ponies

Come on you little darlings, and let's go watch your daddy gather
A thousand head of horses out of grassy Garvin Basin
They are running all together as they have been all this winter
And it is a sight that we may never chance to see again
So let's hurry up the mountain, watch, and sit, and wait there
To see a thousand pretty ponies pouring over Garvin's Rim

The summers for years have been drouthy and hot
Grasshoppers and crickets have eaten the feeds
Still there was grass in the Basin, and the crickets were not
So we leased out its grass for the wintering of steeds

We had dude ranchers cavvies and roundup remudas
And rodeo rough strings all wintering there
On range that was strong—sure the best that there was
In these Montana thirties, all else is plumb bare

It took me and six fellows to get them all gathered
The horses like wild bunches scattered before us
We rode our poor broncs till they tired and wavered
Then roped us some new ones and went on from there

Sometimes our new mounts were good ones and true
Though often as not they'd buck and they'd pitch
But my boys from the Antler are cowboy plumb through
And they rode what they caught—didn't much matter which

A hard day of riding on a bunch of fresh horses
But finally we had them all lined out and loping
Due east toward the trail, and we cut off their choices
Till they headed up here just like we'd been hoping

Now I see my sweetheart, the kids, and they're waving
Even the wee one from there on her hip
I thought that they would like the sight of us gathering
A good thousand horses is a sight worth the trip

Over yonder, see them coming, there's your daddy and he's running
With a thousand head of horses out of grassy Garvin Basin
They are rippling like a river with their manes and tails flying
Flashing, glinting colors—proudest thing I've ever seen
And see his hat it's waving as he comes riding hard and spurring
Leading all those pretty ponies pouring down off Garvin's Rim

Timothy Draw

We pause at the top of Timothy Draw
Look down the country for stray cows
He cocks his head
Stands in the stirrups
Hands on the horn
Relaxed and easy and graceful
He moves with a horse
Like few men can

In one brief, quick space
I love him more
Than I will ever love again

Like passion, but not of sex
Like life without death
Like the nudge and the tug and the sleepy smile
Of a too-full child at your still-full breast
Something that explodes from your toes
But flows through your bones
Like warm honey

More powerful than violence

Far too

. . . Good

To speak of

The Big Lonely

Why is it that
A hundred sections of rock and grass
With absolutely nobody on it
Except you, a horse, and some scattered cattle

Is never lonesome
And sounds like paradise,

But a trailer house
In town, full of closed-in kids
Too many neighbors and too much noise

Is more . . . lonely
Than anything I've ever known?

Ah . . . it is indeed a tragedy
To contain so much open space
In one misplaced
Soul.

What I need is a back-country coyote pair
Just outside
"Go to it, folks"
Drown out the town dogs and . . .

Howl one for me.

Bríghid

In Celtic mythology, Bríghid was the goddess of smithcraft, healing, poetry, and knowledge. Her festival, attended only by women, was celebrated at calving time. (The "í" in Bríghid's name is pronounced "ee.")

Listen to the winds of Spring in Wyomin'
Chinookin' through wet, slow-falling snow.
It wanders, and whispers like sighing women
With secrets to tell of the things they know—
When the calves start comin'.

In the long, dark nights just sit and listen
To the old, old tales that a woman tells
When no cow is in labor, no tail is switchin'.
The best songs come in the calvin' lulls,
When the men are sleepin'.

There flows in our veins the fightin' strains
Of ancient Celtic cattle people,
So here in the West on good grass plains
The souls of the old ones chose to settle,
And claim these prize terrains.

Yet still that old Celt blood flows free
And the timeless tales are sung
Of Patrick, and Finn, and the goddess Bríg—
Bríghid that gracious, warrior one
With the Earth at her knee,

Spear in her hand, crowned as a judge,
Surrounded by herds and poetry,
Goddess of smithy, healing, and knowledge
Three sisters form one trinity—
Become a mystic bridge.

Born neither in, nor out, of a house in the dawn,
Raised on the milk of a red-eared cow,

She speaks to us and her flame burns on
In our minds, our hearts, and our wisdom, now,
Though her virgins are gone.

Our mothers still tend, on calvin' nights
In early Spring, to tell their girls
The lore of birth—the rituals and rights
Of women—and how life hurls
Bliss and pain, joy and frights.

Loving and strong women stand in her shadow
Fierce Bríghids in these lonesome hills—
Women of learning tend their cattle,
Shoe their horses, pound their anvils,
And doctor from saddles.

So here in Wyoming her fires are burnin'
Bríghid, great goddess, she still lives on
Submerged in the secretive womanly learnin'
Now, as then, when the men are gone
And the calves are comin'.

You can die like a frightened whore, or you can live like a worthy huntress.

—AGNES WHISTLING ELK—

SUE WALLIS

Sue Wallis was raised on a cattle ranch in the Powder River Breaks of northern Wyoming and southern Montana. She descends from several generations of ranching folk and rodeo people, a family rich in lore and legend. Her great-grandfather, "Packsaddle" Ben Greenough, grew up in an orphanage in Brooklyn, New York. In 1886, Ben went West and found work as a cowpuncher on the Crow Reservation. He later homesteaded near Red Lodge, Montana, and made his living taking "pilgrims" out on pack trips hunting and fishing.

Ben's five children—Sue's grandparents, grandaunts and granduncles— were known as the Riding Greenoughs for their skill in the rodeo arena. While Sue's grandfather went into ranching, Turk, Bill, Marge, and Alice were all champion saddle-bronc riders and were eventually inducted into the Cowboy Hall of Fame. Having nothing left to accomplish in the United States, Alice went off to Australia and then to Europe, where she rode fighting bulls in the bullrings of Spain.

Since 1992, Sue has been Assistant Program Director at the Western Folklife Center in Elko, Nevada. The walls of her office are covered with rodeo photographs of her renowned family. Her favorite is a picture of Marge and Alice seated behind the bucking chutes, daintily applying lipstick while a curious horse looks on. Sue says her grandaunts were proud to be real ladies and not "rounders" like many women who rodeoed. With "those Greenough girls" as her models in life, Sue has written that she weaves her way between "wild adventure and solid refinement."

Following Greenough tradition, Sue entered the world of rodeo as a child. "I grew up playin' in the dirt behind the buckin' chutes," she says. Her best events were breakaway calf roping and goat tying, contests she often won. "Daddy taught me how to get off a runnin' horse, which sometimes gave me an advantage."

Sue attributes her strength to the women in her family, and to the fact that from an early age she'd proven her ability to do physical work on her family's Wyoming ranch. There was no distinction made between Sue and her brothers; like them, she was a good hand—good enough to further sharpen her skills cowboying on neighboring ranches. Early in life, Sue developed a strong bond with the wide-open landscape in which she was raised. She says that her favorite place growing up was the windblown sagebrush expanse of Jerry Finn Flat, the site of a roundup camp on the old Greenough ranch.

Sue went to high school in Gillette, fifty miles from her family's ranch.

On weekends she and a girlfriend would visit the bars in towns from Gillette to Sheridan, playing pool. Her friend, she says, "ran the tables," a skill the local guys didn't always appreciate. After high school, Sue worked the coal mines of the Powder River Basin, driving heavy equipment.

Born in 1957, Sue had her first child, Isaac, at age twenty. That didn't slow her down. "After my son was born, I went to work coalminin' for Kerr McGee." Before her recent marriage to Rod McQueary, as a divorced single mother she brought up Isaac and her two other children, Megan and Sean Rys, on her own. Like Sue, all are enthusiastic and inquisitive readers. Work and marriage prevented Sue from going to college until 1989, when she went to the University of Wyoming in Laramie and majored in American Studies. She says college was where she found out she could write.

It was Sue's father, now a Wyoming state legislator, who first introduced her to poetry. "When I was a kid," she recalls, "Daddy would take me along when he fed heifers with a team of horses along Bitter Crick. In a loud, booming voice—he was very theatrical—he'd recite Kipling by the hour. The feeding took two days, so I learned a heap a' Kipling." Sue was inspired to start writing limericks. By the time she was twelve, only one had survived. It was about a rose, that's all she remembers. " 'Rose' was a good rhymin' word," she says with a hearty laugh.

One of the most compelling voices in cowboy poetry, Sue is widely known for her skill with both traditional and contemporary forms, and for her powerful recitations at poetry gatherings. In her poetry, she strives for a "clear, strong, positive female voice that speaks to, and for, the feminine concerns in ranching culture." Sue's poems are rooted in abiding ties with the land that she traces back to her ancestry, the Scots-Irish origins of cattle people. "Bríghid," like many of her poems, reflects her fascination with Celtic mythology.

Sue's poems have appeared in several anthologies. In 1991 Dry Crik Press published a chapbook, *The Exalted Ones*, and *Another Green Grass Lover: Selected Poetry* was published in 1994. In addition to poetry, Sue writes articles and short stories, and she has a novel in the works. Recently, in collaboration with Nevada composer Gary Buchanan, she was commissioned by the Northern Nevada Orchestra Association to create a poetic accompaniment for a symphony, *Cattle, Horses, Sky, and Grass: A Sagebrush Suite*, the title taken from one of her poems.

Since early 1993, Sue and her kids have made their home in pastoral Starr Valley, twenty miles from the town of Wells in northern Nevada. The house they now share with Rod, a simple brick-red ranch style, is set back off a dirt road, on the far side of a creek. The home is surrounded by natural springs, the family's source of water.

Each morning at dawn, Sue climbs the hill in back of the house to a large meadow, "to see what the day is gonna be like." Coffee mug in hand, she slowly circles the meadow, stopping occasionally to pluck a wildflower out of the moist grass or to gaze at the sun rising over the snow-covered mountains to the east. This place, she says, reminds her of Wyoming. Soon, Sue and Rod are planning to lease enough land to start a small grass-fed cow operation—a return to the life and the work they know best.

Vess Quinlan

"The sense of place, the sacred, is where people have lived
and worked . . . Once you destroy a culture, you can never get it back."

Sold Out

The worst will come tomorrow
When we load the saddle horses.
We are past turning back;
The horses must be sold.

The old man turns away, hurting,
As the last cow is loaded.
I hunt words to ease his pain.
But there is nothing to say.

He walks away to lean
On a top rail of the corral
And look across the calving pasture
Toward the willow-grown creek.

I follow,
Absently mimicking his walk,
And stand a post away.
We don't speak of causes or reasons,

Don't speak at all;
We just stand there
Leaning on the weathered poles,
While shadows consume the pasture.

The Trouble with Dreams

She followed me to ranches
That were a long way
From anywhere,
Made sad houses smile
When they hadn't in years.

She would sometimes cry
To be so far from family
With only distant neighbors,
Dogs, and me.

A mother's work
Brought less distress;
But still dreams,
An apartment, shopping, movies.
A good safe job
Where cows would not run over me
Or horses fall and break my legs.

We would make new friends
And go to elegant parties.
She would work in a bright little shop.
There would be no more full ashtrays
And dirty coffee cups.
No cowmen to talk of debt and drought
No ripe smell of manured boots,
No Combiotic in the refrigerator
No half frozen calves on the porch,
No dust blowing in the house
And no mud tracked on her kitchen floor.

Now her dream is true;
I write my little poems.
She swims in the pool,
Soaks in the hot tub,

Goes shopping,
And hides the tears
I know are there.

Finally, she asks
If I might find some cowmen
To visit, drink coffee,
Talk about cows, fill the ashtrays,
And track mud on her kitchen floor.

The Cutting Post

A great cedar post
Stands alone and waits
For the men to return
Rebuild the corral
And reclaim a life
Abandoned thirty years ago.

The high desert has been kind
To the items left behind.
Here a bean platter and there
Nearly buried, a broken sheep bell.
Most things were scavenged and reused.
Those left are silent, secretive.

I sit against the great post
Draw circles in the soft dirt
Look down at the long building
That housed the men with families
At the bunkhouse for the single men
And wonder if they were happy there.

I try to hear the shouts of men
And feel the movement of the herds.
I want to see brown faces
And smell sheep-raised dust.
I hear nothing but silence
Feel only loneliness and loss.

I wonder about this silent place.
The road is steep and rough
But in two hours I am in town
Asking old brown men if they know
Of the abandoned headquarters
On the mesa, above the Rio Grande.

"Si," they say, "old Faustine was
Mayordomo there for many years."
I find an ancient man living with
A granddaughter named Semonia who is
Suspicious of me and my questions.

"My grandfather," she says, "is always
Begging me to take him up there
But it is too far and the rocks
In the road would damage tires.
The old man remembers only the good
But his was a hard life that turned
Bright young women into hags
And strong young men into old bent ones
So gringos could drive big cars."
I ignore her taunt and say carefully
That the old ways interest me.
After an exchange of high-speed Spanish,
So high speed I miss most of it
There is agreement.
Faustine may go tomorrow morning.

I am early. Semonia says, "The old man
Has been up since before dawn
Drinking coffee and waiting.
He is excited, like a child.
Just what I need, a missing husband
And a ninety-three year old child."

I am offered coffee. The old man
And I converse in Spanish
Become co-conspirators as we ignore
Snorts and ridicule from Semonia
Whose remarks suggest that we are fools
Who waste time and tires
Trying to steer a pickup into the past.

The old man takes the ride well.
He talks; I listen; we become friends.
I drive to the great post.

"I want to know," I say, "about all this."
"What do you want to know?" he asks.
"All you can remember," I say.

"I cut this fine post myself," he says.
"Had the hole dug five feet deep
And tamped the dirt to be sure.
I smoothed the post with a hoof rasp."

The old man places his hands on the post
Seems to drift back, become younger.
He moves his body gracefully left
And a phantom ewe is sent to the right.
Pivoting on the post his body
Blocks the open passage and another
Is cut into the missing left corral.
"We had ten thousand," he says, "five bands."

The cutting post is polished smooth
Shaped with a gentle wearing away
Where the sheep passed rubbing lanolin
From their wool into the fine cedar wood.
The passage of tens of thousands of sheep
Has made a flowing sculpture of the post.

I draw circles in the dirt
And lean against the cutting post.
The old man rests beside me
And talks of the glory days
When this was a great ranch
And he a masterful mayordomo.
Now I see brown faces
Hear long dead voices
Smell the sheep-raised dust
And feel the movement of great herds.
We stay all day.

VESS QUINLAN

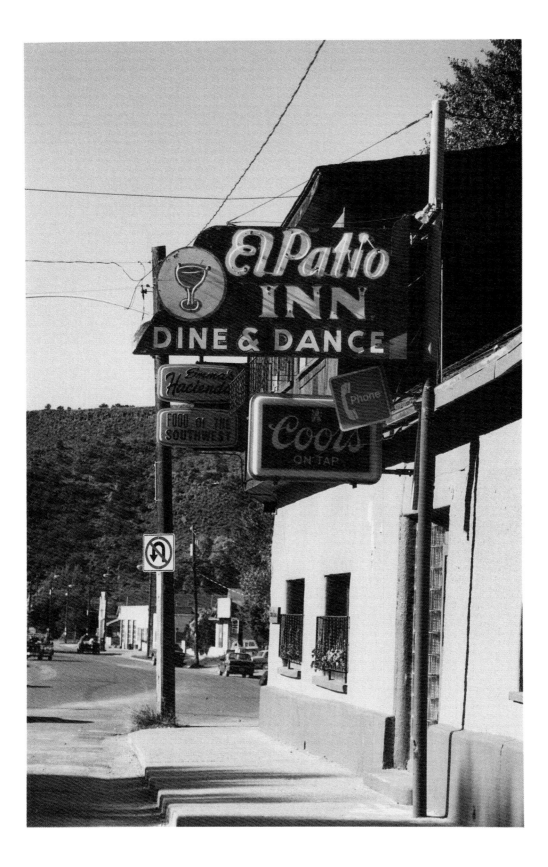

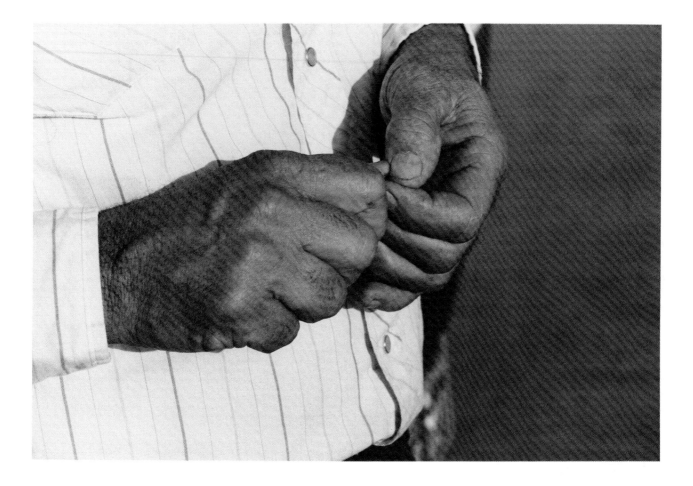

VESS QUINLAN

V ess Quinlan's family goes back four generations in Colorado. His great-grandfather, J. P. Quinlan, came to eastern Colorado in the late 1800s looking for gold. He invested his slim share of the profits from his claims in a ranch near McCoy, at the confluence of Rock Creek and Grand River. A rugged individualist, J. P. was, as Vess puts it, "Irish in a 'Help Wanted—No Irish Need Apply' world."

The history of Vess's family, on both sides, reflects the hardships small ranchers have endured in this century in the West—the subject of some of the poems in Vess's book, *The Trouble with Dreams*. During a cowboy poetry gathering in Grand Junction, Colorado, Vess told me that in the 1930s his grandparents on his mother's side were driven off their land near Pueblo when they became overextended buying breeding stock in the good-times twenties. Much of the ranching country that stretched eastward from Pueblo and south to the New Mexico border was "bought up by Texas oil people in the 1950s and '60s," all but destroying the area's ranch-based communities. "When I was growing up," Vess remembered, "on a Saturday night we used to be able to find a schoolhouse dance. No more."

Vess was born in 1940 in Eagle, Colorado. After high school, he cow-boyed on outfits all over the state. Like his grandfather, Emmet, he was a "driftin' wages cowpoke." He worked the same country as Bruce Kiskaddon, the classic cowboy poet he admires. Later, Vess and his wife, Arla, moved every year as he worked on one ranch after another. "We started on the western slope of the Rockies, near Eagle, where both of us were raised, and ended up on the eastern slope—short grass country." "Quittin' and movin' " is a cowboy trait, he says.

There's a hitch to Vess's gait, the result of a bout with polio as a child. In the days before the Salk vaccine, he spent much of his childhood in and out of hospitals. That was where, at age ten, he started writing stories in the form of poems. "I remembered stories as a way to escape where I was." At age fourteen, he made his escape a reality, running away from home. "Those doctors would've made me a cripple." A self-described anarchist, he's been carving out his own existence, in his own way, ever since.

In 1969 Vess and his family—Arla, daughter Lisa, and sons Justin and Norlan—moved to Alamosa, in Colorado's poorest county. Vess admits, "I had marched way beyond my ability in partnering up with an investor and buying a rundown southern Colorado outfit thrown together from several unmarketable places foreclosed on by the FHA several years before." The ranch is nestled in San Luis Valley, at 8,000 feet, the biggest alpine valley in the world. "It's one of the last places where you can afford to be poor with dignity. Here, poverty protects us."

Vess claims that learning to produce a decent living from marginal land was and is an interesting challenge. And, he adds, "learning to fit into a culture that is in many ways alien to our own is an even greater challenge." (The Valley, like northern New Mexico, was originally settled by Hispanics, who have often viewed Anglos as intruders since the United States annexed Colorado, which had been a part of Mexico, in 1848.) For Vess, part of meeting this challenge is writing what he calls "Leo Stories." Leo was a Hispanic hand who lived in the valley and worked for the Quinlans. Leo, Delfino Jaquez, and other locals told Vess their stories and taught him the ways of their people. From these folks he learned that "it is possible for a great deal of love and respect to exist between individuals, even when there is little love lost between their respective cultures."

Threatened by the relentless "progress" of mainstream white civilization, these old cultures, like ranching itself, are fast disappearing. "Once you destroy a culture," Vess says, "you can never get it back . . . The sense of place, the sacred, is where a people have lived and worked. Go back to where you lived as a child. What's happening there is what's happening to the sacred all over the world."

Those in the livestock culture, Vess contends, "are not simply custodians of the land. We are of the land itself." Yet those who live and work on the land are now an endangered species. Vess claims that today's ranchers face a future akin to what the Indian faced in the last century, except, as he puts it, "our buffalo is water."

Besides being one of the leading figures in cowboy poetry, Vess is an articulate spokesman in the heated debate between ranchers and environmentalists over the care and use of western lands. An advocate for dialogue, he firmly believes that ranchers "should attend every environmental meeting in America. We should be there not to confront or tell 'em how it is, but to make it as rough as possible to look good people in the eye and run 'em off the land."

A few years back, during hard economic times, the Quinlan family was faced once again with the prospect of being forced off their land. But Vess dug in. Unwilling to give up, he sold off the livestock and turned to raising alfalfa. And, to make ends meet, he began driving an eighteen-wheel truck cross-country for the Leprino Food Company, leaving his sons to run the ranch while he's on the road. Though the bankers are still nervous, Vess hopes to quit trucking soon, and to buy back a few cows.

When asked how he handles the long hours on the road, being away from home for months at a time, Vess replied with a sardonic smile, "It makes me miserable, and that helps my poetry."

Henry Real Bird

"The ground, our earth, is your first mother; where you come from,
your blood mother, is your second mother; and the lodge
is your third mother . . . I still talk with my first mother, Mother Earth.
I offer her tobacco and tears from my prayers to soften my heart."

Cowboy Drifter

The most beautiful woman I ever did see
Greets me each mornin' with the star that's light
Spirit of the ground, feelin' of life
In love with a woman
The best I've known
How love has grown
Beyond the stars
With a heart that's good
In your eye, I stood
Way past reflection shadows alive
Cruisin' through my soul feelin' alive
It damn sure seems like walkin' back
From a good bronc ride walkin' on air
To feel no pain walk on air
To feel no pain walk on air

Cowboy drifter ridin' through the pines
Up on the head of Custer Creek
Drop off into Reno
Down Medicine Tail
I'm going home I'm going home
To the grass that's blue on the Little Horn
To the grass that's blue on the Little Horn

The most beautiful feelin' I ever did use
Got me this feelin' that I want to live
Just in your arms from here on out
Got me this dream that I want to be
The dream in your heart from here on out
In the little wind after the rain
Sweet smell of sage in the air
Wind inside, on hills that are high
Rivers tip among am I
This is the place where fantasy blends in reality
And the sky and ground are one
Reflectin' love I'm ridin' gone

You never did lead me on
Reflectin' love I'm ridin' gone
You never did lead me on

Cowboy drifter ridin' through the pines
Up on the head of Custer Creek
Drop off into Reno
Down Medicine Tail
I'm going home I'm going home
To the grass that's blue on the Little Horn
To the grass that's blue on the Little Horn

Red Scarf

Boots and chinks
Silver bit and silver spurs
Eased into the dawn
To walk out kinks
Horse like shiny, free of burrs
Trotted into day
I'm ridin' bay
If you can see the beauty
In the sunset with many colors
I only see the beauty
In the sunrise with many colors
You can find me
In the beauty in the sky
In sunrise and sunset
In the shadow of the sky
Among the stars
If you can see the beauty, in the sky
You can find me, in your eye
With a red scarf on
Boots and chinks
Here I am, I'm ridin' gone
Ground about day
Lookin' for a stray
Red-tail hawk blessed me with his shadow
Clouds peak to my south
Granite to the west
Sheep Mountains and the Pryors
Look their best
Grass full grown
As I stood
In my heart that is good
If you can see the beauty
In the sunset with many colors
I only see the beauty
In the sunrise with many colors
You can find me

In the beauty in the sky
In sunrise and sunset
In the shadow of the sky
In the shadow of the sky
Among the stars

Among Shootin' Stars

Sold bronc saddle
Foreclosed cows
Through the broken pieces
Of shattered dreams
The dreamer wrote this
From the hollowed feeling of a cloud
Above Thompson Creek
In the Wolf Teeth Mountains
When he used to dream
On the road to California
As he watched
The ground turn to mud
From under the chuckwagon fly
As he sat on the tongue
Jingling spur rowels
A howl in coyote cry
Lurkin' in shadows
Left in time
Such is the feeling that I'm

Head over heels in love with the stars
Feeling in the hills among the shootin' stars
Stuck in the rhythm of a northbound freight
To the buffalo jump bars
In the streets and the cars
For just a thumb to catch a ride that's late
I rode on through the gate.

Met up with a feeling
Lost on the road
Wild horse camp feeling
Should've been told
Before this ever was
Pictures of feeling
Stuck in time
Inscription on buckles

Twinkle in chime
Broncs and women, to glass of wine
Brought back by chuckles
Only to hawk the buckles
The truth
is what you know
As to be true
Underneath the snow
Not what you think
As to be true
In sky turn blue.

Head over heels in love with the stars
Feeling in the hills among the shootin' stars
Stuck in the rhythm of a northbound freight
To the buffalo jump bars
In the streets and the cars
For just a thumb to catch a ride that's late
I rode on through the gate.

The return to cowboy wages
Turn back the pages
Thought from where wildflowers grow
And peaceful fires glow
Around teepee rings
Sweet smell of sage
Among the pine
From out of the grass
Appeared some eyes
Nothing'll last
If you believe in lies
Traded dreams
To break at seams
Lost all my tokens
For this economy
Where soft words were spoken
In lost autonomy.

Head over heels in love with the stars
Feeling in the hills among the shootin' stars
Stuck in the rhythm of a northbound freight

To the buffalo jump bars
In the streets and the cars
For just a thumb to catch a ride that's late
I rode on through the gate.

Cowboy up before the sun
Ride through ground shadow
To lope into a run
Where do feelings go
First sunlight on the mountain
On top of Sheep Mountain
Down to above the canyon rims
Dove on limbs
Thought of you since I've been up
To see myself in coffee cup
Back in time with the movement of a horse
Awake to kiss, and I love you
Sweet smell mist, let it take its course
For my heart is two, because of you.

Head over heels in love with the stars
Feeling in the hills among the shootin' stars
Stuck in the rhythm of a northbound freight
To the buffalo jump bars
In the streets and the cars
For just a thumb to catch a ride that's late
I rode on through the gate.

HENRY REAL BIRD

Henry Real Bird, of the Big Lodge Clan, was born on the Crow Indian Reservation of southeast Montana and was raised there "in the tradition of the Crow Tribe, learning of the horse from the right side, the Indian side." All he ever wanted was to ride horses and become a cowboy. He learned to ride as a boy, when his grandfather, Owns Painted Horse, would turn him loose on a horse to gallop across the plains above Medicine Tail Coulee, near the site of the Battle of the Little Big Horn. Each year, in June, he and his family and friends reenact the famous battle from an Indian perspective, on the banks of the Little Big Horn River. It is one way they've found of preserving their culture.

When he was six years old, Hank went to the Crow Agency Public School, adjacent to the battlefield. Standing in front of the school's entrance, Hank told Kent and me, "I didn't speak a word of English before I went to this here school." Today, he said, he would be in the minority. It is a sad sign of his people's loss of their heritage that now only thirty-four percent of the children going into first grade speak the Crow language. But in Hank's family, Crow is still spoken. For him, keeping the traditions of his people alive is vitally important. "We still speak to the earth and the sky and the water and the animals. We follow the four directions in the thought ways of my people."

Hank has cowboyed on the Crow, Cheyenne, and Osage Indian Reservations. In high school he began riding broncs, which he continued through and after college, in both amateur and pro rodeo. He has taught school on the Crow, Cheyenne, and Osage Reservations, and he is currently registrar at Little Big Horn College on the Crow Reservation.

Bill Jones once asked Hank how he got to the place where he was, meaning, how did Hank come to be at the college. Bill says Hank knew that white guys sometimes don't ask what they really mean. This, in the form of a conversational poem, was Hank's reply:

> My grandfather taught me
> the ways of my people
> Of the sweatlodge and Sundance
> But I was raised a Baptist
> Turned Catholic in my youth
> Hung around a lot of Mormons
> Was baptized five times
> So you see I am a believer

I was working on a roof in Dallas
My shoes stuck to the asphalt
And I wore a baseball cap
It was 115 degrees
I did what the white boss told me
Drank warm beer
And wished I was dead
So I prayed to God
Save my life
Take me home
An artist friend bought me a plane ticket
In two days I was home
and in a sundance lodge
Pretty soon everything was all right again.

Hank is a storyteller, and his stories, like his words, gallop as fast as a horse over the plains. Sometimes they seem to move in circles. He can make you laugh until your sides ache, and then, in the next moment, bring tears to your eyes. If you listen closely, you can learn things. When Hank tells a story, he finishes with "That's where I come from." This is something he knows—unlike most of us in the mobile, modern era, who are generations removed from our roots, and from the earth.

Hank's poems, like his stories, sometimes move in mysterious ways. He admits that he tries to shake people up, to "make 'em think." He also startles audiences with his unusual onstage presentations. Standing tall before the microphone, legs spread wide, his body moves in rhythm to his voice as he recites. In a hypnotic, drumbeat cadence, he weaves lines of poetry with chant, pulling the audience into the poems on powerful waves of sound.

When Hank first appeared on the cowboy poetry scene, his poetry and his unconventional performance style were often misunderstood by all-white audiences. Though this made performing difficult at times, Hank refused to change, saying, "Those who can hear the whistling of the water, they hear me."

Hank has published twelve children's books and a small book of poetry, *Where Shadows Are Born*. He sometimes illustrates his poems with striking pen and ink drawings. In an effort to recover and preserve the oral tradition of his people, he has written *The Creation Story of the Crow People, as told by a Traditional Tribal Elder*. The elder was Hank's grandfather. Hank claims to belong, with Vess Quinlan, to a sub-subculture of cowboy poets in the Rocky Mountains and says that he's "really just a gatherer of thoughts."

With his wife Alma, daughter Lucy, and sons John and Jack, Hank lives on the O-W Ranch in the Wolf Teeth Mountains between Rosebud Creek and the Little Big Horn River. The Indian name for their valley is Yellow Leggings, a land of sage, pines, and lush buffalo grass. "That's why we're here," Hank says, "to take care of the grass." He runs a small herd of cattle, including some longhorns, and takes pride in the horses he and the boys break and train. He is passing on his knowhow and his passion for rodeo to his sons. He says, simply, "We follow the movement of the horse." In Crow tradition, the horse, a sign of wealth, is at the center of life. Much as it is for the cowboy.

A man who embodies the traditions of both the Indian and the cowboy, Hank plays a unique role in keeping the ways of each alive.

Joel Nelson

"I still think bein' a cowboy is the highest callin'."

Kings, Queens, and Mountain Kingdoms

A billion points of starlight dot the iridescent sky
And the full moon hasn't quite yet gone to rest
It silhouettes the mountain peaks and mesas standing high
Out above the rocky foothills to the west—to the west
   And the breeze is stirring lightly from the west.

There's sound like rolling thunder though there's not a cloud in sight
It's a sound the urban cowboy wouldn't savvy
While the city folks are sleeping and the morning star is bright
A Davis Mountain cowboy pens the cavvy—hear the cavvy
   See the sparks a flyin' underneath the cavvy.

The roundup time's approaching just like every fall and spring
In the land that's way too dry and rough to plow
Here a handshake's still a contract and the cowboy still is king
The Queen is still a high horned whiteface cow—hear me now
   I said the Queen is still a whiteface mother cow.

There's a cow crew up and ridin' ere the night is even gone
And a heavy frost is sparkling on the grass
In the lingo of the cowboy it's a silver-mounted dawn
And the moon is just now settin' in the pass—up through the pass
   Like a silver concha settin' in the pass.

At the S.P. Railroad's highest point a traveler on the train
Gazes out across the redrock with a look of mute surprise
At a cow herd thrown together on the grama covered plain
And a mountain cowboy sortin' out the drys—cuttin' drys.
   His old gray, he's got his ears back cuttin' drys.

When the Davis Mountain dusk settles down around the hills
And the 'poor-will and the cricket and the coyote have their say
When the calves have found their mommas and their lonesome
   bawling stills
The puncher pulls his saddle off the gray—for the day.
   And the cow camp sure looks good this time a' day.

Men of higher education trudge the archives musty miles
Inspecting every volume as they go
They are searching for the cowboys in the books that line the aisles
They reached extinction ninety years ago—is it so?
Did they sell their saddles ninety years ago?

No! They're up at dawn and ridin' and they sit their horse with pride
Bottom jacket button's loose and hat's on tight
And if judgment day should catch them they will ride out side by side
They'll be halfway there before it's hardly light—hardly light.
While the cocinero's blowin' out the light.

Sundown in the Cow Camp

The hoodie's washed the dishes
And stacked 'em in the box.
The old cook and the foreman
Have wound and set their clocks.

That horseshoe game they're playin'
Hasta shut down in a while,
'Cause that shadow from the outhouse
Reaches dang near half a mile.

Ol' Charlie's got his guitar out;
That Charlie sure can play.
And it's sundown in the cow camp—
It's my favorite time o'day.

We ate at five this mornin'
'Cept the "kid"—he skipped his chuck.
He just couldn't eat for knowin'
That his mornin' horse would buck.

Now the cook has shut the chuckbox lid
And gave the fire a poke,
Throwed some coals around the coffee pot
And lit his evening smoke.

His expression kinda clues you
That his memories have flown
To other camps at sundown
And the cowboys that he's known.

The "kid" has kept a night horse up;
He's down there in the pens;
Just plumb forgot about his feed;
He's nickerin' for his friends.

Those calves we worked and turned back out
Have purt 'neer mothered up;
Just one old cow left bawlin'.
Think I'll have me one last cup.

You can feel the breeze is shiftin'
Like a cool front's on the way.
Glad the sun's been busy warmin' up
My tepee tent all day.

Some cowboys turn in early—
The cook's the first to go—
While the night owls hug the coffee pot
Till the fire's a dull red glow.

You'll hear it all around the fire—
Poems, politics, and song.
Solutions for the price of beef,
Where the B.L.M. went wrong.

That strong and silent cowboy type—
The one you read about—
He's kinda forced to be that way
When the drive's all scattered out.

But he'll get downright eloquent
When the evening chuck's washed down,
And it's sunset in the cow camp,
With the crew all gathered 'round.

Half asleep here in my bedroll,
I can hear those night owls laugh;
But that old cow's stopped her bawlin',
So I guess she's found her calf.

Awakening

We cannot say what drew us here,
What piper's flute, what siren's song
In younger days—another year
While sun was low and shadows long.

Her great high deserts lured us on—
We were but boys when we rode in
To live the life and chase the dawn
'Till evening sun shone down on men.

And nature was our friend and foe
She dealt us pain, she brought us bliss
Our Mother Earth we came to know
Was nurturer and nemesis.

Our cattle graze her hills and draws
Her August grain is rip'ning now.
For horseback men with horseback laws
May she be saved from park and plow.

We've seen her change since we rode in.
We've read her pages as they've turned
And worn our stirrup leathers thin.
We fear the lessons we have learned.

What hands would tear this place apart?
We are not all what we appear!
We can't afford the careless heart
That beat within the pioneer.

And red man's wisdom has been cast
Aside as savage—yet we see
The noble savage doubtless passed
Much closer to His earth than we.

Are we her stewards, foes, or friends?
And who could better serve the earth?
We throw these questions to the winds
And ride toward answers' timely birth.

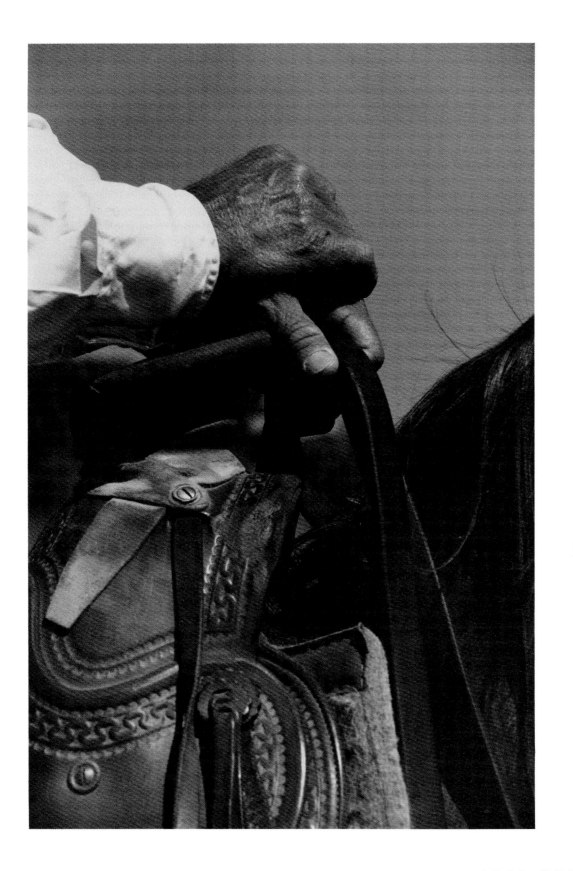

"I reckon I'm a pretty fair cowboy," Joel Nelson says with characteristic humility. (Wally McRae has said that cowboy logic dictates, "The more self-deprecating, the better the cowboy.") Joel's cowpuncher friends would say he's a top hand, someone who, when it comes to handling cows and horses, knows how to be "in the right place at the right time." Joel is a cowboy other cowboys look up to.

Born in 1945, Joel was raised on the Boone Ranch, near Seymour, Texas, about fifty miles west of Wichita Falls. His father, a working cowboy, was Joel's boyhood hero. His earliest recollection, when he was three years old, was "sittin' in front of my dad on his saddle, which had a nickel saddle horn. My dad was showin' me the difference between cow tracks and horse tracks." Joel rode often with his father. When he was six, he got to go along with the cowpunchers as they drove cattle cross-country to the railroad shipping pens at Fulda. "That was the last year the Boone Ranch shipped cattle by rail. After that, they went to usin' cattle trucks . . . I cherish that memory."

Joel admired not only his father, but the other cowpunchers on the ranch. They were his first teachers. "I guess I never did get rid of my worship of cowboys," he says in his slow Texas drawl. Maybe because he was so in awe of cowboys, young Joel didn't aspire to be one himself. Instead, he majored in forestry and range management at Stephen F. Austin State University, graduating in 1968.

After a tour in Vietnam, he returned to West Texas in time for the fall roundup at the 06 Ranch, near Alpine. "All I wanted to do was punch cows." Over the next thirteen years, he cowboyed, broke horses, and eventually became cow boss at the 06. During that time, he married and had a daughter, Carla.

Joel remembers going out "on the wagon" at the 06, a traditionally run ranch where cowboys ate from a chuck wagon during weeks on the range gathering cattle. "I hired cowboys from all over the West to help with roundups—Ross Knox from Arizona, H. A. Moore from Montana, Jeremiah Watt from Canada." At night, he remembers, the men would recite poems, tell jokes and stories, and sing cowboy songs around the campfire. "Those were special times," he recalls with more than a trace of wistfulness in his voice.

In 1991 Joel and his wife divorced and he left the 06. After a summer breaking horses at the Parker Ranch in Hawaii—"the only place I've ever been where the cowboys eat with chopsticks"—he returned to Texas and went to work on the Gertrudas Division of the legendary King Ranch, once the largest cattle ranch in the world. There he met his second wife, Amma Lou, when she brought him her horse, Santana, to train. "We were introduced by a bay stallion," he says.

Close to a million acres of flat mesquite rangeland in the southern tip of Texas, the King Ranch is known for its blood-red Santa Gertrudas cattle and for its superior horses. The King Ranch quarter horse, with the running W brand on its flank, has been highly prized by Western horsemen for decades.

In *The Iliad*, Homer's highest tribute was to call a man a "breaker of horses." For a horseman, to be a "breaker of horses" at the King Ranch is to have reached the pinnacle. Joel learned much of his method of working with horses from Ray Hunt, a horseman and teacher known for his gentle, intuitive approach.

"It took several years before I realized that it was a *philosophy*, not a technique." That philosophy, Joel says, is based on the belief that "the horse is right 100 percent of the time, and always has a reason for what he does. If the horse does somethin' 'wrong,' it's because of what I'm doin.' I try to adjust to him, to get to his mind. My whole approach to handlin' stock is to treat them with consideration and respect."

Joel brings the same consideration and respect to the tradition of cowboy poetry. He wrote his first poems while in Vietnam, in letters to friends back home. After his return, he stopped writing—until he heard about the first Cowboy Poetry Gathering in Elko, Nevada, in 1985. "I didn't realize anybody appreciated this kind of poetry until Elko." The next year he went to the Gathering and found he shared "a bond, a camaraderie, an understanding" with the other poets he met there, many for the first time.

Joel has been writing poems and reciting in his simple, graceful style at poetry gatherings ever since. Leaving the recitation of his own work to others, Joel is known for his eloquent rendition of Buck Ramsey's "Anthem," and for introducing "literary" poems, such as Robert Frost's "The Road Not Taken," to cowboy poetry audiences. He claims Frost's poem could be about a lot of cowboys he's known.

Though he sometimes experiments with open forms, Joel reveres the classic metered and rhymed style reminiscent of early cowboy poems. Following cowboy poetry's oral tradition, he often composes and memorizes poems horseback; "Awakening" existed only in Joel's head until he finally wrote it down for Waddie Mitchell.

At the 1992 Cowboy Poetry Gathering in Lewistown, Montana, Joel was introduced by rancher Gwen Peterson as "the kindest man I've ever met." Joel personifies the strong and silent cowboy image, yet his friends know that his toughness is accompanied by instinctive decency and a droll sense of humor.

Wary of the derogatory criticism cowboy poetry has sometimes received, Joel calls himself a cowboy *and* a poet. "I feel strongly about what I do, about the cowboy way of life, and I try to express that in my poetry." Joel says he's developed a whole new set of heroes: cowboy poets.

Drummond Hadley

"Through the men who have lived and cowboyed here, through their stories and poems, the land becomes a home for the people."

Juan's Last Trail

There's old Juan walking along the ridgeline
    from Mexico Route 2 through the border fence,
then down the rough side of the canyon to the Escondida Camp
    where he hoped his friend Walterio would be waiting.

Tortillas in a sack, a half-filled bottle of tequila.
    Old heart walking, centuries singing,
dry times, the rangelands and wetback trails,
    his own people, Sonora, Mexico.

"Where are you headed Juan?"
    "Where there's work to do," he'd say.
Mexican vaquero following traces of cattle trails drifting through
    those blue Peloncillo Mountain rangelands to find work in America.

Humming of flies along that winding path,
    trembling side-oats seeds . . .

"*Mira*, there," says Roberto, "look past those mesquite leaves."
    Faded Levi's, tan shirt, sombrero by the cliff-rock.
"Where the trail climbs the ridge, do you see him?"
    A hawk goes gliding low over Juan's bones.

Sunlight and the rains, summertime, the worms,
    odor like a cow dead about four weeks.
Grease from his body turning the side-oats grasses brown.
    Grease, coyote, lightning, who knows?

Early fall clouds rolling over the ridgelines,
    our bodies, clouds, dry falling seeds.
Pretty quick a man disappears in these winds
    and the creeks and the mountain sands.

Old Dust in the wind drifting now on this Guadalupe Canyon Trail—
    "Where are you headed Juan?"
"Siempre tengo mi camino en la punta de mis pies.
    Always my way is before me," he said.

    "Only the tips of my feet know where I will go."

Alma de mi alma

A Song of the Vaqueros of Mexico*

El sauce y la palma se mesclan con calma.
Alma de mi alma que linda eres tu . . .
The willow and the palm, they
gently touch each other.
Alma of my soul, soul of my soul,
how beautiful you were . . .

Alma born about 1953 to Don Cruzita Alonzo,
    vaquero in the Cañon de Dimas,
where the swallows come nesting by the red cliffs
    in the springtime, Sonora, Mexico.

Where do the swallows go passing with the west wind,
    where do they nest for a while, and then go?
When she was a young girl her mother didn't want her
    so took her to town to Doña Petra.

Where do the swallows go passing with these west winds,
    where do they nest for a while, and then go?
When she was sweet sixteen Doña Petra didn't want her
    so she went to live with her Uncle Peru.

She was shot through the heart by Peru's jealous wife,
    she's buried in the cañon at El Ranchito.
Where do your hates, and your jealous loves go?
    Who are we here . . . wanting to know?

                Who are we here . . . wanting to know?

Shy, whirling Alma, dancing your young-old eyes
    the carousing vaqueros chased all night
till the sunlight lit their camp on the town street
    between the roundup jefe's house and hers.

*Stanzas in italics are sung with guitar accompaniment

Como un águila bajando a un lepe
Roberto bailó con las señoritas in Agua Prieta.
Like an eagle dropping down on a doggie calf
Roberto danced with the senoritas in Agua Prieta.

Where will the old Earth take you dancing through the starlight
whirling you on and on while she goes?
Where will the old Earth carry us dancing through the starlight
whirling us all on and on while she goes?

Danced her through that old white house where she lived, one room
adobe mud, the other of cardboard, and rusting pieces of rattling tin,
where Petra served us frijoles and carne
as though we'd come driving steers along the dusty trails as kings.

Whirling you on and on while she goes . . .
whirling us all on and on while she goes . . .
West from the San Bernadino River, through Gallardo Pass we rode
in the dusk light, lost two steers in the night time.

Rode on again another day into Agua Prieta,
through dirt streets, and Mexico kids
running by the sides of the road, throwing rocks at stray steers
until we came to the border corrals.

Then with tequila, and corridas floating through the cantinas,
and the women and the songs, we forgot the dust, the wild cattle,
the cold of the mornings, the winding trails, and changed the town
to some whirling place we didn't remember or know.

Where do those nights and the singing in your memories
and the crossing of these valleys and the sandy rivers go?
Where do those nights and the singing in our memories,
and the crossings of these lands and the sandy rivers go?

And the vaqueros who rode whistling
in those soft, dark eyes
while the swallows circled, and drifted in the winds
calling by the red cliffs in the cañon de Dimas in springtime?

Where will those loves, and your laughing black eyes,
and the winding river go?
Who are we here wanting to know,
who are we here wanting to know?

Song of the WS Ranch
Colfax County, New Mexico

SINGING WINDS

    Drift, keep drifting on over the land.

WANDERER

    Got a job cowboying on the W.S.

    Oh you gotta be the same as the wind, or the water,

        or the scattered grasses,

    for one man to move above three hundred cows

        gently across these open plains.

SINGING WINDS

    The sounds of the words in your language,

        like a field of grasses, brown, and gold, and blue, and green,

    stretching like the plains across the open country,

        stretching like your mind when you reach out your hand.

    Or the trickles in the tan dirt where the water's run through,

        or where the earth is cracked up from the sun, and cold,

        and winters, and summers, and the nights . . .

WANDERER

    O beat, beat, beat, gusts a' wind

        on the blue grama grass on the plain . . .

    O beat, beat, the sounds of your voice on the plain . . .

    The squeak of the shanks of the loose-jawed bit,

        and where the reins are fastened on metal rings,

    the whirr of the cricket in the dun horse's mouth,

        the whirr of black and red grasshopper wings

    rising and falling, above the silver grasses,

        juniper trees, piñon trees and the oaks,

    and the shadow of a hawk drifting in the grass

        in the soft thud, thud, of the unshod hooves

        'cause I use him on the plain,

        and not much in these mountain rocks.

    And the ching, ching of the rowels in the spurs

        when they brush against the limbs a' the brush,

mixed with the wind in the piñon trees,
     mixed with the wind in the silver-red grass,
mixed in the breath of the Earth's opening lungs,
     mixed in the quivering seeds a' the grass,
     and the windmill spinning, and spinning, above the plain.

DRUMMOND HADLEY

"I couldn't do this now without everything that came before," Drummond Hadley says in a Missouri drawl spiced with the cadence of the Southwest borderlands, where he has lived for over thirty-five years. He is referring to his acquisition of the 321,000-acre Gray Ranch in southwestern New Mexico. In early 1993, the newly formed Animas Foundation, which he heads, bought the Nature Conservancy's crown jewel. This was at the behest of local ranchers, who feared the development that would accompany the Conservancy's plans to sell the Gray to the U.S. Fish and Wildlife Service. Lying on the U.S.-Mexico border, the Gray Ranch is 500 square miles of the last uninterrupted ecosystem of its kind left in the American Southwest. The trail that led Drummond Hadley—poet, cowboy, and rancher—to this ground-breaking event is as unusual as the man himself.

Born in 1938, Drum spent his childhood near Sappington, Missouri, on the outskirts of St. Louis. Early on he abdicated any claim to his mother's family business, the Anheuser-Busch Companies, Inc., in favor of pursuing lyricism and cowboying. His mother and Busch uncles had raised him to ride and rope on farms near his boyhood home. During his teens, Drum cowboyed for his uncles in Wyoming.

While earning undergraduate and graduate degrees in literature at the University of Arizona, he studied and wrote poetry, eventually coming under the tutelage of the eminent American poet Charles Olsen. At age twenty-one he published his first poems.

In the 1960s he traveled the literary landscape with poet comrades Gary Snyder and Philip Whalen, with whom he retreated for a time into California's Sierra Nevada. Later, he and Snyder continued their quest in Mexico. It was there that Drum began to seek "knowledges that grew from the lives of men and women living in frontiers and vast expanses."

A few months later, he shoved his saddle and bedroll through the international fence, walked south until he reached the headquarters of Rancho San Bernadino, and signed on. The vaqueros took him to Los Chirriones, a cow camp, where he stayed for three roundups. He has spoken of those years spent roping and branding with men so graceful they could dance from one side of a corral to the other on the backs of milling steers. Drum found that the ways of the vaquero encompass more than their unequaled skills as trackers and ropers of wild cattle. "It's a way of being," he says.

Working as a drifting cowboy, he set out to record the knowledge of this borderland cowboy culture, framing the poetry he could hear in the voices of the people. According to Drum, the pure horseback societies that still exist in the Sierra Madres "carry something that we may have lost: an intimacy with land, weather, water and animals, and what that intimacy imposes on human beings."

For over two decades, Drum has lived on a ranch in a rocky canyon that straddles the Arizona-New Mexico line, ten miles from the Gray Ranch. The Guadalupe Cattle Company can only be reached by four-wheel-drive vehicle over twenty-seven arroyo crossings leading up Guadalupe Canyon from Arizona. Drum and his wife, Terry, recently installed solar electricity, but communication with the outside world is limited to a cellular phone in Drum's truck, which can be used on a nearby ridgetop to reach a repeater sixty miles away. In this rugged country, Drum Hadley has forsaken literary circles and achieved formidable isolation.

Of the connection between his chosen lifestyle and writing poetry, Drum has said, "Isolation gives people plenty of time to dip into themselves. If you go horseback into huge spaces, there's not a lot to do but think about things."

Drum's seclusion was challenged by his fateful purchase of the Gray Ranch. This turning point in his life possessed an element of destiny. Like the strands of a rawhide riata, the ways of knowledge he'd acquired in the processes of cowboying, ranching, and poetic storytelling were now converging. Just as he completed a book of prose poems he'd been writing for twenty years, celebrating the borderland he loves, he established a foundation dedicated to preserving both that ranching culture and the wild spaces it depends on.

In late September, I drove seven hours from Santa Fe to the Gray Ranch, in what is known as New Mexico's boot heel. Kent was to visit a week later, at gathering time. Drum greeted me in front of the modest ranch house that serves as headquarters for the Animas Foundation. Though he looked more like a college professor than a cowboy—he once taught poetry at the Naropa Institute in Boulder, Colorado—there was a glint of the wild in his eyes.

Soon we were in Drum's Land Rover, driving south. From the 8,600-foot summit of Animas Peak (the entire range lies on the ranch), down to the immense grassland, virtually no human presence is felt here, save for a few cattle water tanks and an occasional windmill. The objective of the trip was to inspect the results of a lightning fire in June that burned 23,000 acres. Along with the Nature Conservancy and rangeland specialists, Drum believes in making use of prescribed and wild fires to reduce woody plant species and thus restore the natural grasslands.

With us was Roberto Espinosa, a long-time vaquero compadre who appears in Drum's poetry. As we drove through a continually changing landscape, the two conversed in Spanish—soft, melodious tones that echoed the rhythms of the poems. They told stories and looked toward the far mountain ranges and remembered places where they had cowboyed together twenty-five years before. Drum pointed to a jagged line on the horizon: "That's where Roberto and I hunted in 1969 after the roundup that ended in the border town of Agua Prieta, the subject of 'Alma de mi alma.' "

The rutted road wound upward. The results of the fire were impressive: lush grass had sprouted between the blackened skeletons of mesquite and juniper. We passed a group of Chihuahuan pronghorn antelope, local to the area, grazing along a slope, and, further, on, the black forms of javelina— wild collared peccaries closely related to the domestic pig. On a high ridge the road cut through sand dunes, an incongruous sight. Drum stopped the car. Below us was the vast, primordial expanse of an ancient lake bed. To the south, where the Sierra Madre rose in a blue haze, lay Mexico.

From the back seat, Roberto spoke quietly. Drum translated: "He says you wouldn't see a place like this anywhere else on earth."

This richly textured land, its people and the two countries they live in, have become this literate cowboy poet's source of inspiration. Drum Hadley, who refers to poetry as "heightened language," listens to the language of the natural world as well as to human voices. He hears poetry in the songs of the wind, the water, and the scattered grasses, and in the wise words of an old vaquero.

"You never know," he says, "where or how the unknown will appear."

The Photographs

⊱≺≈≈≈

Buckaroo trappings
Vietnam still life
Silver belly hat

San Luis, Colorado
Hands
18-wheeler—Tracy, California

Pages 167 to 171

Henry Real Bird
Medicine Tail Coulee—Little Big Horn, Montana
Hank and son John, O-W Ranch—Yellow Leggings Valley
Hank in the Wolf Teeth Mountains
Real Bird Palomino

Pages 183 to 187

Joel Nelson
King Ranch, Gertrudas Division—Kingsville, Texas
A breaker of horses
Done for the day
Tools of the trade

Pages 199 to 203

Drummond Hadley
Drum and Roberto Espinosa
Fall gather at the Gray Ranch—southwestern New Mexico
Swing rider
Southwestern gear

Coda: Horseshoes, Gray Ranch

Acknowledgments

Devoted thanks to my partner in life, Heidi Wehmeyer, and to my parents, Fred and Peggie Reeves. I also wish to thank Leslie Ann Kossoff of Hi Fi, Inc., in San Francisco, California, who was able to decipher my cryptic notes and directions and print the photographs exactly as I would. I owe my work in this book to all the poets who allowed me to interrupt their lives and who took me in for a few days. I do not feel that I "took" these photographs; I believe that each poet gave them to me.

Kent Reeves

Editor's Acknowledgments

Among the rewards of doing this book are the many people who lent assistance and encouragement along the way. In particular, my thanks to Katy Peake, who helped bring the book into being; Meg Glasner of the Western Folklife Center; Robert Sheldon, Nick Lyons, Inge Morath, Barbara London, Peter Weismiller, Pepa Devan, Anthony Power, and Marie Dern; and to my other dear friends for their loving support.

Special thanks to my partner in cutting this trail, Kent Reeves. Kent's spirit of collaboration with the people and the places portrayed in these pages is best summed up in the words of Linda Hussa: "He saw what was important to us and, with grace and kindness, photographed."

My deepest gratitude to the twelve poets who shared their homes, their lives, and their work. I carry you all in my heart.

Finally, thanks to Lisi Schoenbach at Norton, for her special assistance, and to my editor, Carol Houck Smith, for seeing something in this book and for her faith in me.

Anne Heath Widmark

Permissions

A number of the poems in this book appear in print here for the first time. Other poems are hereby gratefully acknowledged to their authors and publishers:

The following poems were first published in *Dry Crik Review:* "The Blue Filly," by Linda Hussa; "Life and Times," "For Woody," and "For Souls," by Rod McQueary; and "Storm Front" and "My Grandfather's and Father's Horses," by Shadd Piehl. All poems reprinted with permission of the authors.

"Upstream," "When the Redbuds Come," and "Chagoopa Plateau" are from *Hung Out to Dry*, by John Dofflemyer, © 1992, Dry Crik Press; "The Sierra's Spine" was first published in *The Redneck Review*, Winter, 1993. All poems reprinted with permission of the author.

"Song of the WS Ranch" is from *Strands of Rawhide*, by Drummond Hadley, © 1972, Goliard/Santa Fe; "Juan's Last Trail" and "Alma de mi alma," © 1993, by Drummond Hadley. All poems used with permission of the author.

"Under the Hunter Moon," by Linda Hussa, was first published in *Graining the Mare: The Poetry of Ranch Women*, Teresa Jordan, editor, © 1994, Gibbs Smith Publisher. "In This Moment" and "A Birth" are from *Where the Wind Lives*, by Linda Hussa, © 1994, Gibbs Smith Publisher. All poems reprinted with permission of the author.

The conversational poem quoted by Bill Jones in Henry Real Bird's profile is reprinted with permission from *The Dude from Hell*, by Bill Jones, © 1992, Bill Jones, Publisher.

"For Souls" and "For Life," by Rod McQueary, are from *Blood Trails*, by Rod McQueary and Bill Jones, © 1993, Dry Crik Press. Both poems reprinted with permission of the author.

"Things of Intrinsic Worth," "Little Things," and "I Never Rode the Judiths" are collected in *Cowboy Curmudgeon*, by Wallace McRae, © 1992, Gibbs Smith Publisher; "Reincarnation" was first published in *It's Just Grass and Water*, by Wallace McRae, © 1979, Outlaw Books. All poems reprinted with permission of the author.

"Sundown in the Cow Camp," by Joel Nelson, was first published in *New Cowboy Poetry: A Contemporary Gathering*, Hal Cannon, editor, © 1990, Gibbs Smith Publisher; "Kings, Queens, and Mountain Kingdoms" and "Awakening," © 1993, by Joel Nelson. All poems used with permission of the author.

"Towards Horses," by Shadd Piehl, was first published in *Aluminum Canoe*, Spring, 1993; "Winter Breaks" first published in *Pemmican*, Winter, 1994. Both poems used with permission of the author.

"Sold Out," "The Trouble with Dreams," and "The Cutting Post" are from *The Trouble with Dreams*, by Vess Quinlan, © 1990, Wind Vein Press. Reprinted with permission of the author.

"Anthem" is reprinted with permission from *And As I Rode Out on the Morning*, by Buck Ramsey, © 1993 Texas Tech University Press; "Bonnie Trina" © 1993 by Buck Ramsey, used with permission of the author.

"Cowboy Drifter," "Red Scarf," and "Among Shootin' Stars" are from *Where Shadows Are Born*, by Henry Real Bird, © 1990, Guildhall Publishers. All poems reprinted with permission of the author.

"A Thousand Pretty Ponies," "Timothy Draw," and "Bríghid" were first published in *The Exalted One*, by Sue Wallis, © 1991, Dry Crik Press; these poems and "The Big Lonely," are collected in her *Another Green Grass Lover: Selected Poetry*, © 1994, Dry Crik Press. All poems reprinted with permission of the author.

"Staircase" is from *Roughstock Sonnets*, by Paul Zarzyski, with photographs by Barbara Van Cleve, © 1989, The Lowell Press; "Words Growing Wild in the Woods" first appeared in *CutBank 40*, Spring, 1993; "Luck of the Draw," © 1993, and "A Song Moment for Ian Tyson," © 1994, by Paul Zarzyski. All poems used with permission of the author.

Books by the Contributors

John Dofflemyer

Dry Creek Rhymes, Dry Crik Press, Lemon Cove,
California, 1989
Sensin' Somethin', Dry Crik Press, 1989
Black Mercedes, Dry Crik Press, 1990
Muses of the Ranges, Dry Crik Press, 1991
Hung Out to Dry, Dry Crik Press, 1992
Cattails, Dry Crik Press, 1993
Maverick Western Verse (editor), Gibbs Smith Publisher,
Layton, Utah, 1994

Drummond Hadley

The Webbing, Four Seasons Foundation, San Francisco, California, 1987
Strands of Rawhide, Goliard/Santa Fe, Santa Fe, New Mexico, 1972

Linda Hussa

Diary of a Cow Camp Cook, Sagebrush Press, Cedarvile, California, 1990
Where the Wind Lives: Poems from the Great Basin, Gibbs Smith Publisher,
Layton, Utah, 1994

Rod McQueary

Blood Trails (Bill Jones, coauthor), Dry Crik Press, Lemon Cove,
California, 1993

Wallace McRae

 It's Just Grass and Water, Outlaw Books, Bozeman, Montana, 1979
 Up North and Down the Creek, Outlaw Books, 1985
 Things of Intrinsic Worth, Outlaw Books, 1989
 Cowboy Curmudgeon and Other Poems, Gibbs Smith Publisher,
  Layton, Utah, 1992

Vess Quinlan

 The Trouble with Dreams, Wind Vein Press, Ketchum, Idaho, 1990

Buck Ramsey

 As I Rode Out on the Morning, Texas Tech University Press,
  Lubbock, Texas, 1993

Henry Real Bird

 Where Shadows Are Born, Guildhall Publishers, Fort Worth, Texas, 1990

Sue Wallis

 The Exalted One, Dry Crik Press, Lemon Cove, California, 1991
 Another Green Grass Lover: Selected Poems, Dry Crik Press, 1994

Paul Zarzyski

 Call Me Lucky, Confluence Press, Lewis & Clark College, Lewiston, Idaho, 1981
 The Make-Up of Ice, University of Georgia Press, Athens, Georgia, 1984
 Tracks, Kutenai Press, Missoula, Montana, 1989
 Roughstock Sonnets, The Lowell Press, Kansas City, Missouri, 1989
 The Garnet Moon, Black Rock Press, University of Nevada, Reno, 1990